It's NEVER TOO LATE

It's NEVER TOO LATE

CREATING THE LIFE OF YOUR DREAMS

CHRIS & DEBBIE ATKINSON

NEXT CENTURY
PUBLISHING

It's Never Too Late
Creating the Life of Your Dreams

Published by Next Century Publishing
Las Vegas, NV

www.NextCenturyPublishing.com

ISBN: 978-1-62903-828-5
Library of Congress Control Number: 2015933191

Printed in the United States of America

Dedication

By the time Debbie and I met, her parents had already passed away, but even though I never had the pleasure of meeting them, our dads had met each other. You see, Debbie and my sister, Diane, were born just 24 hours apart at the same hospital. We often imagine our dads standing side by side at that hospital window in the maternity ward gazing at their daughters. Now Debbie's dad was from Brooklyn so I can only imagine how cool that conversation was: a true Texan and an Italian (Brooklyn) man, both bragging.

Over the years, as Debbie has shared many stories with me of her childhood and life before we met, many similarities have been discovered about our parents. I am positive her parents also lived by the rule of "It's never too late."

Throughout my life, growing up making mistake after mistake, from over a dozen times in jail and almost a dozen treatment facilities for alcohol and drug addition, from multiple car repossessions to home foreclosures and even bankruptcy, one thing has always been true: my parents never, not one single time, ever gave up on me.

So I would like to dedicate this book to my wife's loving parents for helping her to become the lady she is today, while also thanking my parents for one major statement they made to me while I was in my early 20s. They said and I quote, "You obviously do not realize this today, but you were not put on this earth to be worthless. Go discover your passion and you will not fail."

Mom and Dad, I love you. I love you for your care, your thoughts, your prayers and your compassion. It is because of you that I am who I am today. May God continue to bless you and everyone who ever has the honor of being in your presence. Thank you for never giving up on me. Thank you for believing in me even when I could not believe in myself.

Dedicated to:
Joseph & Frances Curcio and
Duncan & Marie Atkinson

Contents

Introduction

You weep for all your childhood dreams

that have vanished with the years.

You weep for all your self-esteem

that has been corrupted by failure.

You weep for all your potential

that has been bartered for security.

You weep for all your talent

that has been wasted through misuse.

You look upon yourself with disgrace and you turn in terror

from the image you see in the pool.

Who is this mockery of humanity staring back at you

with bloodless eyes of shame?

— **Og Mandino,** *The Greatest Miracle in the World*

Chris

I remember the first time I read those words. It was as if they were being spoken directly to me, directly to my soul.

I felt the pain of vanished dreams, lack of self-esteem, lost potential, and wasted talent.

I knew all too well what it was like to stare at myself with shame because I had a lot of things I was ashamed of. A failed marriage. A child I couldn't see. Bankruptcy. Foreclosure. Addiction.

At the age of thirty-eight, I was a failure in the eyes of society and in my own eyes. The future, what there was of it, looked bleak; and I didn't know what to do or how to do it.

This is a story of transformation—of renewal—of redemption. I'm not telling it so that I can feel good or be proud of myself, but because I want you to know that what I learned and what I did to turn my life around is available to you as well.

It doesn't matter where you are in your life—you can have a new beginning. You can start over. You can have the life of your dreams.

I don't know exactly what that life looks like for you. For me it started with being able to pay my bills and go a month without having my electricity shut off. Gradually, my dreams grew, and as they grew, so did my confidence that they could and would come true. My dreams expanded to include finding the love of my life, my soul mate; having a wonderful relationship with my son; creating a lifestyle that allows me to have the satisfaction of a job well done as well as the time to enjoy the rewards.

I now have the life of my dreams, and I know you can too.

Helping you achieve that dream is one of the reasons I get up each morning.

As Og Mandino goes on to say in his masterpiece, *The Greatest Miracle in the World*:

Still I love you and I am with you now,

through these words,

to fulfill the prophet who announced that the Lord

shall set his hand again,

the second time,

to recover the remnant of his people.

I have set my hand again.

This is the second time.

You are my remnant.

Chris

I am a remnant who got a second chance. You can be one too. All you need to do is make today the first day of your new life. Once you take this step, everything—and I do mean everything—will change. Remember, it's never too late!

Debbie

When I was working as a registered nurse, especially in an emergency room and in a poison center where so many decisions were a matter of life or death, I used to pray that I would do the very best job I could. One prayer, written by Rev. Larry L. Jackson, really captures what I felt about nursing:

Holy One, as we begin this day, I ask for Your guidance.

With Your divine hand, inspire, lead and give Thy wisdom.

Throughout this day, may Your grace be ever present

in this healing place.

Bless our team, our hospital, our unit, as we gather

to help those in need,

Let not Your help be far away.

We seek Your strength and ask that You give spirit as

we make decisions for the good.

God of love, teach us to give our best, to speak

with love and act with courage

May we be good stewards of all the gifts You have given.

Amen.

Although I am no longer working as a nurse, the words of this prayer continue to be an inspiration to me. They are the way I want to live my life for the rest of my life—being part of a team that helps those in need, giving my best, speaking with love and acting with courage. These are the ideals that I keep in front of me every day.

You may think that you have already lived the best years of your life and that all the good times are behind you. I fully understand. Ten years ago, I felt the same way. I was just hoping to get to retirement age and have enough money to make ends meet. If you feel that way, let me assure you that there is an even brighter future waiting for you—no matter your age. I truly believe the words of C. S. Lewis, who wrote *The Chronicles of Narnia:* "There are far, far better things ahead than we have left behind."

One of the reasons I wanted to write this book is because I know how incredibly blessed I am to have been given the opportunity to create a life I never dreamed could be mine, and I want to encourage you to believe the same thing can happen for you.

Do you want to go on living the way you have been living, or are you willing to do what it takes to have the life of your dreams? It's up to you. What will you choose?

Wishing you the best first day ever,

Chris and Debbie Atkinson

Chris's Story

Chapter One

Most couples look at their newborn baby and think about the wonderful life their child will have. They hope for health, happiness, and success. No couple looks at their newborn and wishes, "Oh, I hope he is going to grow up to be an addict, have a failed marriage, go bankrupt, and still be living with us when he is in his thirties." Certainly my parents never wished that, never even thought that, on the clear, bright October morning in 1966 when I came into the world. And yet all of those things happened—and worse.

From a solid middle-class beginning, I managed to fall into all the traps that destroy lives. I'm just lucky that I survived. But looking back, I now realize that, while all the wrong turns, dead ends, and sinkholes of life seemed like just so much bad luck, they were the result of my own bad choices and decisions. While I wanted—and did try—to blame everything on everyone else, the only person responsible for my life is me. I am the one who made the choices, and I'm the one who lived out the consequences.

But it's more than that. All the hard things I experienced—from alienation from my son to jail to bankruptcy—helped shape me into the person I am today. So, as odd as it might seem, I am truly grateful for everything I had to go through in order to be where I am right now. In fact, if you were to ask me what I would change about my life, I'd say, "Not a thing!" Not because I would want to relive my past, but because it was the path that led me to the life I live today ... the life of my dreams.

In the Beginning

Every story has a beginning, and mine starts in a little town called Texas City, Texas. Located on the shore of Galveston Bay, just across from Galveston Island, Texas City is a petroleum-refining center. If people know anything about it, they may know it as the site of a major explosion in 1947 that destroyed the port and nearly demolished the entire city. But that was all before my time. To me, it was just home. It was a great place for a kid to grow up, with a lake, streams, and the ocean nearby.

My parents moved there as soon as my dad graduated from the University of Texas. Dad was born in 1927 and had lived through the Great Depression. That experience shaped him, as it did so many others of his generation; so he took the first job offer he received after his college graduation, which was at Amoco, a gas and oil refinery in Texas City. He made one vow to himself and my mom—that all of his children would graduate from the same high school. This was important to him because he had moved thirteen times before he graduated from high school, and he was determined not to have that happen to his family.

But more than that, he wanted his family to have the best life possible. He worked hard to support us, as did my mom who owned a catering business and a Hallmark card shop. While my brother and sisters and I weren't given a silver spoon, we did have everything that a family would need as well as a few luxuries like nice vacations.

I can honestly say that I never wanted for anything when I was growing up. But that didn't stop me from heading down some very dark roads.

The Root Issue

In retrospect, I think some of my issues began because I was one of the smallest kids in my class when I was growing up. My parents thought they were doing me a favor when they started me in school just before my sixth birthday, but I was a small child and I'm still a slight man today. Of course, my size doesn't excuse my actions, but I did let it negatively affect my choices and decisions.

As a young boy, my size didn't make any difference. My friends and I just loved to be outdoors, playing any

19

kind of sport you can imagine. We were skateboarders, and we loved to ride bikes. We played every sport possible. It didn't matter if it was football, baseball, basketball, or Frisbee. If it was outdoors and some kind of sport, we loved it. We lived close enough to bike to the bay and go fishing. Then when I was twelve years old, I got involved with flying remote control airplanes and was thrilled to watch those models take flight.

In those days, it was safe for kids to be outdoors until dinnertime. My mom had a big, old dinner bell she'd ring, and when we heard it, we knew it was time to head home. We would stay out until the very last minute, and then when we heard that bell, we'd race home as fast as we could. I lived as close to an ideal childhood as you could get. I had friends, I enjoyed good times, and I was loved by my parents.

The Love of the Game

Although I really liked all sports, I think my favorite was baseball. The year I was ten, I was the pitcher for our team and my dad was the coach. I knew we were having a good season, but I was more interested in playing the game than paying attention to the statistics. Then, when the season was over, my dad showed me the books he had kept. Of the games we played that year that I pitched, I had nine wins and no losses and I'd batted .650 for the year.

That began my lifelong love of the sport, and later on, when I was in the deepest despair, it was a mitt and a ball that helped me see what pitches in life I was turning into strikes because I wasn't even bothering to take a swing at the ball.

Taking Responsibility

I begin my story with this background because I want to make it very clear that I had a good start in life. Some people blame their parents and their upbringing for the trouble they have later in life, and I'll admit that for a long time I tried to do just that. But as I said, I now know that the mistakes I made weren't the fault of my parents. My parents were—and are—great people who did their best to raise a child the right way. Everything that went wrong in my life was the result of my own choices, my own actions, and my own doing. Here is a paraphrase of a quote from one of my favorite books, *The Secret*: I know that I am responsible for everything that has happened to me because of what I did or didn't do or what I was or wasn't thinking—but most of all because of the choices I made each and every day.

That's one thing I want you to know and understand. Playing the victim and blaming others for what has happened to you will never get you where you want to be in life. It's only when you accept responsibility for your actions and realize that no one is responsible for your life but you that you can begin to change.

I've learned that lesson now, but it was a long time in coming. However, the good news is that *It's Never Too Late* to make a change. I know … because I've done it.

> *"You are not a victim. No matter what you have been through, you're still here. You may have been challenged, hurt, betrayed, beaten, and discouraged, but nothing has defeated you. You are still here! You have been delayed but not denied. You are not a victim, you are a victor. You have a history of victory."*
>
> — **Steve Maraboli**, *Unapologetically You*

Today I forgive myself for all my past mistakes and accept full responsibility for my future actions.

Chapter Two

My story began to take a turn when I was eight or nine. About then, my dad got a promotion at his job, and his company started sending him all over the world. We wouldn't see him for months at a time. In fact, I spent one Christmas in Poland because that's where my dad was working. When he would come home to Texas, it was for only two or three weeks at a time.

Feeling Different

That's when his absence and my size began to affect me. I remember starting to feel different, insecure. I was used to Dad coming home from work and talking to Mom for a while, then changing his clothes and meeting me in the backyard with a bucket of balls. He'd hold the catcher's mitt in place, and it was my job to pitch those balls and hit that mitt every time. It was our routine and our time together. When I was practicing with my dad, everything just seemed right.

But when his job responsibilities changed and he was no longer available every night after work, my self-confidence gradually faded. Bit by bit, day by day, that inner glow grew dimmer and dimmer. I began to notice that I was smaller than some of the other guys on the team, and I lost confidence in myself. I began to see not what I had in life, but what I didn't have. I stopped being grateful and started to focus on what I lacked.

Descending into the Valley

At that point, I started down a path that I now realize I was fortunate to escape with my life. I don't say that lightly. I mean it. I am fortunate that I am still alive. So many others have gone down that same road and ended up in the obituary columns. I know that I'm one of the lucky ones; I'm one who was able to find a way out of the hell I had created for myself. It's not because I'm special or because I have some extraordinary talent. When I say that if I can do it, you can too, I mean it. No matter where you are in your life, no matter what you have done in your past, you can change your life, starting today. You can climb your own personal mountain.

But before I can tell you about the path I took to the top of my mountain, we have to go back to the valley where it all began.

My First Drink

I can still see myself ... just a scrawny little kid, looking for something to make me feel like I belonged. That afternoon, I was going to play football on the corner lot with some of the guys. A lot of them were bigger than me, so I felt scared because of my size. My dad wasn't around, but I knew where he kept his Scotch, so I dragged a chair over to the cupboard, pulled myself up, and grabbed the bottle. I'm not sure if I just wanted to feel connected to him or if I thought the drink would make me stronger, but I can still remember that first drink. I can still feel it burning down my throat and landing with a hot splash in my stomach, but more than that I remember how it made me feel. All of a sudden, things didn't look so hard. Those guys didn't seem so big. I didn't feel so alone. So I took a couple of big gulps of that Scotch and headed out. By the time we were playing the game, I had absolutely no fear and the fact that I was the smallest kid didn't bother me at all. I had plenty of "liquid courage" running in my veins!

That's where it all began—with a bottle of Scotch and a corner lot football game. Of course, I didn't drink all the time at first. I didn't need that extra boost of confidence daily. Besides, I knew my mom and dad would catch me if the bottle was empty, so I learned to refill it with water just before Dad would come home from a trip. At first, I would only take a drink when I was feeling scared or insecure or worried.

At age ten, I didn't have all that much to worry about, but then I entered adolescence and that's a tough time for any kid, especially one who is concerned about his size and his abilities.

Down, Down, Down

When I was about fourteen or fifteen, I started running with a group of older friends who had easy access to beer, which made drinking a whole lot easier. My friends always just let me drink whatever beer I wanted to drink. About that same time I tried marijuana for the first time. Because I am a person who can get addicted very easily, it didn't take long for me to fall into the habit of getting high or drunk every day before I was even in high school.

Amazingly, I was able to keep my addictions hidden from my parents until I was sixteen. The day they found out is seared into my memory. I had been working on the car. Back in those days, you would pour some transmission fluid in the carburetor to help clear it out. Then you would have to drive the car. While you drove, the fluid would create an enormous cloud of white smoke that puffed behind the car for a few miles. So one Saturday afternoon I poured in the fluid, and my buddy who was helping me jumped in the car with me to drive it out.

It wasn't just an ordinary drive because we were also smoking a joint. Now you need to understand that I had tinted my windows and taken the window cranks off the car so someone didn't accidentally roll down the windows and mess up the tint. So, lo and behold, there was a policeman behind us that we couldn't see because of the window tint. After following us for a couple of miles, he made his way around us and pulled in front of us to make us stop. Well, there we were, two teenagers with a lit joint in our hands, but unable to roll down a window to make the smoke disappear. Naturally, he took us right to jail.

To be more exact, he took me to jail because I was sixteen. My buddy was fifteen, so they held him in the little waiting room and called his parents, who came and picked him up. I sat there for another hour before my parents arrived to get me out of jail. That was the beginning of their knowing I was heading down the wrong path as fast as I could go.

The First Chance to Change

Looking back, I can see that being taken to jail was the first chance I was given to correct my behavior before too much damage had been done. I believe that we are given chances for change throughout our lives, but we don't always take them. I didn't take this first chance, and I didn't take the next hundred either.

What about you? Are you being given a chance now that you are ignoring? If you are, pay attention. The sooner you make the decision to change, the better your life can become. You don't have to wait until you are on your last chance to change!

> *"No one can make you feel inferior without your consent."*
>
> — **Eleanor Roosevelt,** *This Is My Story*

I know that I am uniquely created, and I have a gift to offer the world by my presence. Today I make an effort to be the best person I can be.

Chapter Three

I was given a chance to make my life very different, and I didn't take it. In fact, I didn't even recognize it as a chance for change because all I got was a little slap on the wrist. The ticket I ended up getting was for possession of paraphernalia, which I figured wasn't any big deal. My parents were disappointed, but they figured I'd learned my lesson. Unfortunately, the only lesson I learned was not to get caught smoking a joint in a car with tinted windows.

Busted for a Bar Stool

Life went on as it had before, with my getting high before school and hiding it from my parents. About a year later, my buddies and I were in Galveston and had been drinking real hard—so hard that we were kicked out of the bar. On the way out, we stole one of the barstools and threw it in the car with us. We did it just for the heck of it. We never dreamed that a barstool would be our downfall, but the bartender called the police. About five miles from the bar, the police caught up with us and took the whole group of us to jail. We were charged with public intoxication and held in a cell for five or six hours. Finally we were released, and we drove ourselves home.

Once again, I had been given a chance to change, but I just didn't take it. In fact, I didn't even recognize it as a chance. My parents were upset, but it was just one more little slap on the wrist; and they didn't think that I had a serious drinking problem. It's not that my parents didn't care—they did—but they just didn't understand the seriousness of my addiction. No parent wants to think his or her kid has a big problem. I just laid low, and after a few weeks, things pretty much went back to normal. At least, back to what I considered normal at the time.

Another Chance to Change

I really want to stress that what happened in my life wasn't my parents' fault. Everything that happened to me was the result of my own choices—including the choice not to take advantage of the opportunity to change when it would have been relatively easy.

But I didn't change, and a few months later, after a high school football game, my buddies and I were driving back to our town. We were cruising down the road about eighty miles per hour when the cops pulled us over. I was driving, and I was undeniably drunk. I couldn't walk a straight line. I couldn't say the ABCs. I couldn't do anything the cops asked, so they took me to jail for a DUI— driving under the influence.

By now my parents were rightfully upset, but they also wanted to help and protect me, so they hired a lawyer and got the charge changed to public intoxication. At the time, I thought it was another victory since there would be no DUI on my record. Public intoxication wasn't that big of a deal, or so it seemed to me.

My parents didn't really know what to do, but they wanted to keep me off the roads, so my mom sat me down and said, "Listen, if you're going to drink, drink at home." I can remember thinking, *Wow! I just got permission to get plastered as long as I do it at home.* The next Sunday there was a big football game on TV, so I asked my mom if she was absolutely sure I could drink at home. She said I could, so my buddies and I took a TV from the house, ran an extension cord into the backyard and prepared to watch the game. We had a couple of ice chests full of beer, and we sat there all afternoon just drinking and having a great time.

When the game was over and I started back into the house, my mom looked at the backyard littered with beer cans and then at me and said, "Really? This is how you behave?" She just couldn't believe that we had sat there and gotten roaring drunk in the backyard. "This is the first and the last time you're going do that," she said. Again, I was being given a chance to change, and again I ignored it. I just got angry and told my mom she didn't understand and stormed off.

They say that things come in threes. If that's the case, this was my third chance to turn my life around before things got really bad. Unfortunately, I tossed this chance away too. For the next ten years, I would live in anger and denial, spiraling further and further down into a pit of despair that I was digging for myself—one bottle and one joint at a time.

Upping the Ante

From the time I was a junior in high school, not a day went by that I didn't do something to get high. If it wasn't drinking, it was smoking marijuana—every single day of my life. I still thought that I was holding my life together, until just before my senior year.

I had fallen in love with baseball as a kid, and I still loved the sport. But when I was seventeen, I had to have elbow surgery that resulted in my being unable to play that year. Baseball was the one thing outside of getting high that gave my life meaning and purpose. When it was taken away from me, something changed inside. I no longer cared about anything in life except getting high. When I was high, the pain and meaninglessness of my life disappeared for a little while. I could forget about everything that made me sad or angry.

It was about this time that I got into more than just marijuana and alcohol. I started using all sorts of drugs, including meth and cocaine. The only thing I never did was stick a needle in my arm. The only reason I didn't do that was because I was a diabetic taking four shots of insulin a day, so I refused to stick myself with yet another needle. I recognize the irony: being a diabetic who had to give himself regular shots was the only thing that stopped me from shooting up as an addict.

Wasting a Life

I know my parents tried to warn me about the dangers of drugs and alcohol. However, speaking from experience, that's where people go wrong: they try to tell their kids that alcohol and drugs are harmful, but they do little to steer their kids away from these. Yes, they are—and I'll be the first to admit it—but there is a reason that people drink and get high: it takes away their pain for a little while. When you are high, you aren't thinking about your future; you aren't making goals or dreaming dreams. You are simply numbing the present enough so that you can go on another day. Sometimes, especially when you don't think you have anything to live for, all the warnings about the evil of drugs and alcohol don't compare to the feelings you get when you are under the influence. However, just living from day to day with no goals and no dreams is no life. In fact, it is a complete waste of time.

> *"Tell me, what is it you plan to do with your one wild and precious life?"*
>
> — Mary Oliver

Today is the only day I have. The past is over and the future has not yet arrived. I will live every moment to the fullest, and trust in the process of life.

Chapter Four

I started college in the fall of 1983 at Lamar University in Beaumont, Texas. It's a small school located about ninety miles east of Houston and about twenty-five miles west of Louisiana. At the time, you were supposed to live in the dorm for at least your first year, but I had no intention of doing that and told my mom I didn't want to live in any stupid dorm. Now, the real reason was that I didn't want anyone curtailing my drug and alcohol use. I knew if I was in a dorm, someone would be bound to discover that I was getting high every day, and I had no intention of stopping—college or no college.

By then I was a master at manipulation, so I looked up a guy who had graduated from my high school who was a student at Lamar. There was a loophole in the student code that said if a student was living with a relative, he didn't have to live in the dorm. So I called this guy my "cousin" and moved into his apartment with him.

Match Made in Heaven

As far as I was concerned, he and I were a match made in heaven. He loved marijuana the way I loved beer, so we could both use our drug of choice without our parents finding out. I thought it was an absolute stroke of luck and the best thing that could have happened to me.

The first few weeks were great. Then, the fact that I had started first grade a year early caught up with me. Texas had recently changed the law to lower the legal drinking age to nineteen. When I was turning eighteen that October, my friends all wanted to celebrate my becoming "legal" because they assumed it was my nineteenth birthday. All the old feelings—the ones of not being good enough, of being too young or too small, or of not being the person everyone thought I was—flooded back. When I had to admit I was turning eighteen, I again became that little kid who hoped to find confidence and courage in a bottle of Scotch. I felt the need to crush those feelings, so I began to drink more and smoke more—anything to make me feel like I was someone.

Breakdown

About halfway through the first semester of college, sometime in November, I broke down. I went home to my apartment after a class and called my mom to say, "I can't take this. I can't handle life. I can't be away from home. I just can't do it. I can't make this work." To her credit, she didn't tell me to pack up and come home. Instead, she talked to me for a bit and told me to call back the next day. The next day I was feeling better, so we made the decision that I would stay at Lamar, but I would talk to a psychiatrist. Now I didn't really think that talking to anyone would make a difference, but I was willing to go along with the plan as long as I didn't really need to change. Looking back, I see this as yet another chance I was given that I refused to accept.

I'd stop for a six-pack on the way to the doctor's office and have a couple of beers before my appointment, figuring the doctor couldn't tell that I'd been drinking. When the session was over, I'd get back in the car and pop another one, thinking it unlikely that anyone would be watching me from the window. I was sure I was safe from discovery.

I figured that since my parents knew I was seeing a psychiatrist, they would think I was getting help and wouldn't be on my case. I told myself that my parents would think I was staying sober and going to school, so I could just go ahead and do my own thing—which was drinking and getting high. I was very good at hiding my addiction from them, and they really didn't probe too deeply. So I kept drinking and drugging my way through my second semester and then returned to Texas City for the summer.

On the Job

My dad got me a job at an oil refinery, and I worked four days a week, ten hours a day. I had to be out at the site by about 6:00 a.m. because our shift was 7:00 a.m. to 5:00 p.m. I managed to stay sober during the day, but by 6:00 p.m. I was out with the boys. After work I would come home for just long enough to shower and eat, then go get drunk. I'd get home about 1:00 or 2:00 a.m., catch a few hours of sleep, and then go back to work. This was my schedule throughout that summer.

At the time I thought I was getting away with something, but the only thing that was getting away was my life and future. I'd like to say that I turned my life around after that summer, but I still had a long way to go before I hit rock bottom—nearly twenty more years.

How much time have you wasted already? How much more time will it take before you decide that today is the first day of the rest of your life? What is holding you back from making that decision? Believe me, nothing you have now can compare with what is waiting for you!

"*What seems to us as bitter trials are often blessings in disguise.*"

— Oscar Wilde

No matter what it seems like, I know that things work out for my greater good; so today I will be grateful for all that has happened to me.

Chapter Five

That next fall I didn't go back to Lamar. Instead, I transferred to a small junior college so I could live at home. Once again I thought I had lucked out. I was riding back and forth to college classes with a buddy from high school who had a big party van. He liked to do all the stuff that I liked to do besides drinking, so we got along famously. Looking back, I realize that I had two separate groups of friends. One group just drank and didn't touch drugs. The other group did both. So I started splitting my time between the two groups so that I could "fit in." That was always a theme of my life—trying to "fit in." The one place I really felt like I fit in was with my buddy. He was just like me, so we drank on the way to school and smoked on the way home. It seemed natural and normal to me to be either drunk or high. The few times I was sober, the old demons came back to haunt me, and I'd reach for a bottle or joint as fast as I could.

Bottle in My Boot

My entire sophomore year passed in a haze, and summer rolled around again. I went back to the refinery for my second summer. I told the guys at work that I was diabetic and being out in the sun all day was killing me. I was having low sugar reactions every day, so the company gave me an office job. There I was, twenty years old, in the office with the chief instead of out in the field breaking my back. He and I got the mail and read the blueprints and did "office work." Now wouldn't you know, he ended up being what I thought was a "cool dude." He showed me how to put a bottle of whiskey in my boot every morning. I came to work with my bottle, and he didn't care how much I drank. So I worked all day with my bottle of whiskey and went out every night. Before I knew it, my entire life—every single moment—revolved around getting a buzz. As soon as I woke up, I would take a drink, and the last thing I did before I'd go to sleep would be to take another one. Well, I really never fell asleep. I just passed out every night. In the heydays of my drinking, I would drink at least a case of beer plus an entire bottle of vodka every single day. When I say that I'm lucky to be alive, I'm not exaggerating. It's really a miracle that I didn't die.

First Treatment Facility

On some level, I knew that I was heading pretty far down the path of addiction. So in 1987, when I was twenty-one, I agreed to go to my first treatment facility, a place called Baywood Hospital. I stayed there for twenty-eight days. I went through the program and was introduced to the twelve-step fellowship of Alcoholics Anonymous (AA) at that time. During the month I was in the hospital, I had all my therapy sessions during the day and then attended AA meetings at night. Once again, I'd like to say this was the turning point, but it wasn't. However, one thing did happen that stuck with me and made a difference years later when I really did hit the bottom.

There was a guy in the hospital with me. I'm not sure how old he was, but he probably was in his mid-thirties to early forties. He said to me, "How old are you?" When I told him I was twenty-one, he said, "You're too young to be here." At the time, I didn't think much about it, but it did stick in my mind.

It's hard to admit, but the second night after I was released from treatment, I went to an AA meeting, then stopped at the store and bought a six-pack. I had been sober for a month, but after two beers, I was feeling good again, feeling like "myself" again. Of course, feeling like "myself" meant being drunk.

Back to the Beginning

It was like that month of treatment never even happened. By the next day, I was back to downing a twelve-pack. It was about this time that I started to have thoughts of suicide. Both of my parents were out of town, helping take care of my older sister who had cancer. They were more than a thousand miles away, so I felt like I could do whatever I wanted—and what I wanted to do was drink. Or die.

When my parents figured out what was happening, they called the insurance company and one thing led to another until I returned to the hospital. I stayed only a week or so before going right back to my old ways. At the time, I was seeing a therapist. She came to visit me and said, "You know, you don't really need to be here, do you? You know what to do to stay sober." I wanted out of there, so I of course told her what she wanted to hear. She got me out of the hospital, and I went right back to drinking.

It's true, I did know what I needed to do to stay sober, but I literally couldn't do it. There was a part of me that wanted to get clean, but there was another part that just wanted to keep on drinking. I think that's true for a lot of people. It isn't until what you want becomes stronger than what you have that you are ready to make the changes that will reform your life.

I enrolled at a different junior college near our house and got a job at the bookstore in an attempt to always be around older people who were positive. Despite that, I could not for the life of me stay sober. I would start to drink before I'd go to work at the college bookstore, and I kept an ice chest stocked with beer in my car. I would go out during my lunch break and drink some more.

"Return the Favor"

At the time, I had an older cousin in Austin who had been sober for probably two decades. She came down to Texas City to visit my parents and said to me when she arrived, "You've got to return the favor." I didn't have any idea what she was talking about, but she reminded me that, years before, she had taken me to an AA meeting, so now I had to take her to one.

My heart just sank. I knew I wasn't following the program, but I didn't feel like I had a choice, so I found a meeting and took her to it. After the meeting, my cousin realized that I hadn't been clean or sober, but she didn't degrade me or act as if she was disgusted with me. We went back to my house and talked for hours about life, the dangers of drinking, and what I had been doing to my life. I decided right then and there to turn my life around. I knew I was being offered a chance, and I reached for it.

Life started to get better. I got married, and my son was born on October 1, 1991. I don't know if it was the thought of being a parent or just that I figured I could handle a few drinks after so many years of being sober, but the day after his birth, I was right back to drinking again.

Five Steps Back

You've probably heard the expression "Two steps forward, one step back." Well, in my case, it was "two steps forward, five steps back." Almost instantaneously, I went from being sober to being a drunk. I did everything I could to hide it, but the fact was that, despite all my good intentions and all my months of sobriety, all it took was one drink for me to throw away all my resolve.

Sometimes I wonder what might have happened if I had never taken that one drink. I'll never know, but if you have some temptation in your life that you think you've conquered, don't for one minute think that it can't grab hold of you again. Life is made up of minute-by-minute decisions. Right now, make the right decision. You know what it is, so have the courage to do what you need to do. Don't waste another moment of your life.

Make the choice to change.

Remember, it's never too late.

"It's never too late to start over!"

— **Lynne Gentry,** *Reinventing Leona*

**I have all that I need to make a new start.
Today I choose to do just that.**

Chapter Six

I might not have been able to stay sober, but I did have one skill. It's not a skill I'm necessarily proud of, but over the years I had honed it to perfection. If there was one thing I could do and do well, it was manipulate people and things. I was a master manipulator.

Crazy Thinking

I had managed to get a $13,000 loan from the bank, and I had opened up a car stereo/alarm/paging business. I wasn't making much money at it, but it had the great advantage (in my mind) of not having anyone to keep track of my drinking. I shake my head now, but I even turned down a good job just so I could keep drinking. There was a Shell refinery in town where I had turned in my application. I was called in for an interview, and then I was called back for a second interview. They were paying $40,000 a year, which was good money to me at the time. But I knew working for Shell meant not only a drug test to get hired initially, but also random testing after I was employed. I also knew that no one was going to drug test me if I owned my own business, so when I heard the message on my answering machine that I had been hired by the Shell refinery, I just hit the delete button. I never told a soul that I had been hired.

It might sound crazy, but my thinking was crazy at the time. All I wanted to do was be able to have the freedom to drink whenever and whatever I wanted. Accepting a "regular" job would have been the end of my so-called freedom.

Doing It MY Way

So, I opened up the pager business and the first few months were good, but the business itself never really took off because, let's face it, work got in the way of my drinking. My parents wanted to help, but I just pushed them away. I told them, "I can do this. I've got it covered." The reality was that I had all kinds of pagers out there that I wasn't being paid for because I just wasn't billing. Because I wasn't billing, I wasn't getting any income; but as long as I had enough money for beer, I didn't really care.

One of the saddest things about this period of time was the damage to my life. It was early 1992 when it all came to a head. I had left work a little early and gone home. My wife caught me out in the kitchen with a bottle of whiskey upside down in my mouth and, for her, that was it. So I called Mom and Dad and went back to live with my parents.

Saved by Love

One last thing happened. Though my marriage had failed, I was babysitting our son one night. Despite the mess I was making of my life, I loved my son then and I love him today. I honestly believe it was that love that saved my life.

I had stocked up at the liquor store, so I put our son to bed and started drinking. About midnight I was sitting on the couch with a little .25 caliber pistol in one hand and a bottle in the other. I cocked the gun and stuck it in my mouth. I could feel the pressure on my finger when, all of a sudden, my son cried out. He was hungry, so I put down the gun and went to take care of him. I got him fed, changed, and back to sleep before returning to the living room. I was scared by how close I had come to ending it all, so I called a guy I knew from the AA meetings. He came right over to the house, even though it was 1:00 a.m.

You'd think that experience would have put me at the bottom, but unfortunately it didn't. I know it seems hard to believe, but even coming that close to suicide, I wasn't ready to quit drinking.

Change Is an Inside Job

I now understand that no one and nothing outside of yourself can make you change. Change has to be an inside job. You have to reach the point where you yourself are not just willing, but completely committed, to change. You can't allow yourself an escape clause; you can't say "tomorrow" or "the next day." You have to totally and irrevocably commit yourself to making the change right now.

What are you waiting for? I can assure you that whatever you are waiting for is never going to arrive, so you might as well stop waiting.

> *"The world as we have created it is a process of our thinking. It cannot be changed without changing our thinking."*
>
> **— Albert Einstein**

I believe that the answer to my problems is right before me, even if I am not seeing it yet. I open my mind to all possibilities.

Chapter Seven

I like to tell people that it's never too late to make a change in your life. I also like to add that it's never too late to start over ... and over and over ... until it finally sticks.

Making a Decision

I decided that August 18, 1995, was the day Chris Atkinson was going to get clean and sober for good. I knew that it was going to work this time because it was my dad's birthday. I had always secretly blamed him for my problems. I thought if he hadn't taken that job, if he hadn't spent so much time away from us, if he hadn't worked so many hours—but it was always if *he* ... never *me*.

I was also fed up with my life. My marriage had failed, I'd been in jail a few more times for DUI, and I'd lost my business. When I woke up that morning, I knew it was going to be the best day of the rest of my life. I went to an AA meeting and got totally involved in the program. I mean I absolutely worked the program and all of its steps. I got clean and sober. In fact, I was on so many localized committees all over the state of Texas that I began to be pretty well known as someone who had worked the program and succeeded. After I spent a couple of years clean and sober, I started being asked to speak all over the country.

Now, I'm a simple person. It doesn't take scientific knowledge for me to make a decision. If it feels right, it feels right. It doesn't take an act of Congress or a parting of the Red Sea; if something just feels right, I can run with it. That's exactly what it was like that August. It was like the stars had aligned and everything finally fell into place.

A Birthday Night

A year later, I brought my parents to a meeting with me because it was what AA calls a birthday night. People would talk for a few minutes before calling people forward to get a chip for being sober one year. I wanted my parents there with me that night so I could wish my dad a happy birthday since his birthday was the day of my sobriety.

It really was a new beginning. My sobriety brought us all closer together, and things started to look up for me. I got a good job at a car dealership in our hometown, and I became the assistant manager of the aftermarket department, in charge of car and truck accessories. I finally got to a point where I started to feel like I was somebody. I was important. I had a job and a life again.

I got involved with a buddy of mine who liked to go to the gym, so I started to work out. I continued to attend AA meetings, staying clean and sober. I met a great girl and started dating. I got promoted and then promoted again. Life just seemed to be great.

A Happy Ending?

Cue the soaring music and break out the Kleenex. I finally had my happy ending, right? Not so much.

Pretty soon I stopped going to AA meetings because, well, I didn't need them anymore. My pride began to get the best of me again. The downhill slope started one evening when my girlfriend and I were in the kitchen. She was cooking and said, "I fixed chicken and green beans. What else would you like?" I looked at her and said, "I would like you to leave right now."

That was it. She packed up and left. The way I saw it, my world was opened up again to do whatever I felt like doing. Life was grand. I was single, with no responsibilities. My parents had given me my grandmother's house, so I had no house note. They paid the electric bills, and the only thing I had was a $400-a-month truck payment. What could be better?

So, I fell right back into the trap once more. After being clean and sober for nearly seven years, I started drinking again. And just like every other time, all it took was one drink and I was hooked. I can remember standing out on the back porch being completely disgusted with myself that I was back to drinking a case of beer and some vodka every day. I said to myself, "You know what, Chris? You've been to eight treatment centers. You can quit this anytime you want." The only thing was that I really didn't want to badly enough.

Crack Addict

You may not think it possible, but here's where my story gets even darker. The only thing that allowed me to stop drinking was crack cocaine. I got hooked the very first time I tried it. I got hooked really, really bad. It changed everything about me instantly. I became a moron. I became an ass. It just grabbed hold of me and refused to let go. My new normal became smoking crack for seven straight days with no sleep, then just crashing for probably a day to a day and a half. Then I would finally wake up and eat something. I was a diabetic who needed four insulin shots a day—but on crack cocaine, I couldn't eat. So I just totally destroyed my life.

I quit my job and cashed in my 401K that had just over $9,000 in it. I spent that in three days. I started stealing everything I could. I was stealing from my parents. I would steal my dad's tools and pawn them. I was doing whatever I could to get my next hit. I was right back where I had started. No, that's not quite true. I was in a much darker, much worse place than I had ever been in before; and there was nothing to stop me.

You may think you've done so many bad things in your life that you can never recover, never start over. I want to assure you that if I can come back from the hellhole I had dug for myself, you can too. I won't lie to you; it will take decision, determination, and dedication. But it can be done. I did it, and I know you can too!

"In life you need either inspiration or desperation."

— Tony Robbins

I know that I can always start over. It's never too late for a new beginning.

Chapter Eight

As I look back, the beginning of the end was when I started to get pulled over for DUIs. I didn't see it at the time; but, as they say, hindsight is 20/20.

It was a sorry pattern. The police would take me to jail. My parents would get me out of jail. I would get pulled over and taken to jail. My parents would get me out of jail. This, along with the drugs, was becoming a regular occurrence.

My parents sold the house I was living in and moved me in with them. I'm sure they thought they could keep a better eye on me if I was with them more of the time, but I just stole their ATM card. I would sneak out of the house and ride a bicycle five miles to the drug supplier's house.

I literally could not stop using. Cocaine had a hold on me like nothing before. Finally, one night I planned to break in to the place where I used to work and steal everything I could, alarms or whatever. I didn't care what I took. I just wanted anything I could carry out and sell.

Trapped in My Own Hell

It was early evening, and just dark enough that I didn't think I could be seen. I was leaving the scene of the crime through the garage door. As I looked over my shoulder, there was a policeman walking up to me with a flashlight. I picked up the tools I had on the ground and slowly walked over to my truck. I put them in the front seat and started to drive down the alley. At the other end of the alley was another policeman. He was standing outside his car with his flashlight pointed at me. I actually slowed down to veer over so I wouldn't hit him, then I just punched it.

I was in a four-wheel-drive Nissan extra cab truck with a four-cylinder engine and I thought I could outrun the cops. And I did try my best. The freeway was nearby, so I drove up on it and headed back to my hometown. Then I took an exit and began zigzagging through the streets. I would go a block or so and turn left, then a quick turn to the right. And as I flew through that neighborhood, I just kept hoping I'd lose the cops.

At one point, I took a wrong turn and ended up heading into the parking lot of a closed office. Their electronic gate was down, so I had to back up and do a U-turn. By this time, the two officers had me cornered with their cars, but I was so sure I could get away, I just squeezed between them and headed back to the freeway.

All of sudden, as I made a right turn, a third policeman was right in front of me. He pointed his gun at me and unloaded his entire 9-mm clip. The bullets shattered the windshield, and one very nearly hit the gas tank. Still, I wasn't ready to give up. I kicked out what was left of the windshield and just kept on driving like a madman.

I managed to keep ahead of the police for another ten minutes or so, but then I rolled the truck down into a culvert. Miraculously, I wasn't injured. I sat there for a second and then shoved open the door and started to run. I had just broken into a run when, all of a sudden, I had a flash of sanity and just stopped dead in my tracks right there. I dropped my hands to my sides and waited for the police to catch up to me. I was done running. Done running from the police, done running from my life, done running from me.

Naturally, I was arrested and hauled off to jail on charges of theft and endangerment of a police officer. The last time I'd been arrested for a DUI, my dad had said to me, "If you ever go to jail again, do not bother calling." I knew he meant it, so I just hunkered down in jail and waited to see what would happen.

About three days later, the guard told me I had a visitor, so I went down to the visitor's center and there were my mom and dad.

The first thing out of my mouth was, "I didn't call!" Even though I had disappointed them so many times, it was important to me that they knew I had respected that wish. They knew I hadn't called; they had read about me in the newspaper.

Jail or Probation

This time, though, there wasn't anything they could do to get me out. I had two one-million-dollar bonds on my head because of the charges of aggravated assault on police officers. But they did hire an attorney, and after four months in jail, I was given a plea bargain choice. If I pled guilty, I could do three years in a state prison or ten years on probation.

During those four months in jail, something had begun to change deep within my soul. For the first time, I wasn't thinking about how unfair life was to me or how badly life had treated me. I began to think about how I had hurt my parents and, even more important, how I had hurt my son. I realized that I wasn't going to be able to mend bridges if I spent three more years in a cell, so I chose the ten years of probation.

On my way out, one of the sheriff's deputies said, "Boy, you made the stupidest mistake. I guess I will see you again real soon." At the time, I thought, *No, not this time. Not ever again.*

On the way out of the jail, my dad had me stop at an attorney's office and sign bankruptcy papers. Then he took me directly to a treatment facility. The old me would have been thinking about how I could manipulate the system and get back to my old way of life; but this time, I recognized that treatment was my only option.

Love Changes All

I'm not sure that I had completely made up my mind to change when I walked out of jail, but it was love that finally made the decision for me—the love of baseball and the love of my son. These two loves came together in a way that I can only describe as a miracle.

The very next day, my parents brought my son to see me, along with a baseball and two gloves. The facility let us go to the field next door to play catch. We tossed a few balls back and forth, and then I just broke down. I sat down right there in the field, with tears streaming down my face. I looked at my little boy, and in that moment, I felt something change within me. All the other times I thought I'd made the decision to change, but deep down I always knew I was holding something back. I always had a little mental escape clause.

Not this time. For the first time in my life, I made a promise that I knew I had to keep. I told my son, "I'm going to be your dad, a real dad, from now on."

The date was July 28, 2001.

I want you to take a minute now and notice the date that you are reading this. If you choose, today can be the start of the best days of your life. It's all up to you. So what are you going to do today?

"Today is the first day of the rest of your life."

Yesterday is gone. Tomorrow has not yet arrived, so I choose to live fully and completely today!

Chapter Nine

I'm not going to pretend that everything was ideal from that moment on. I still struggled with my addictive tendencies, and I know that I'll have to stay vigilant for the rest of my life. But I knew that I had to keep my word to my son.

It took until February before I was out of treatment and getting my act together. By then, I had a little house and was doing whatever I could to earn money. My biggest problem was that I couldn't get a job because I couldn't find anyone who would hire me.

No One Will Hire a Former Addict

I don't blame them. Taking a risk on a former drug addict with felony charges isn't any HR department's idea of a wise move. A perfect example was Brink's Home Security.

A headhunter had found me and said that with my experience in electronics, I would be able to get a job without any trouble. I thought, *Yeah, right*, but I was willing to let them try. They got me an appointment with Brink's. I walked into the lobby of the building where they were hiring and sat down with twenty other people. The recruiter called my name first, and I was thinking, *Oh, man! Wouldn't it be amazing if they really did hire me?*

The interviewer brought me to his office and just looked at me. He stared at me, not saying anything. I didn't know what to say, so I just sat there. He stared at me a little longer, then tore up my application and let the pieces fall on his desk. He shook his head and said, "Whatever made you think that I would let you go into people's homes? You, with your history and record?" He then pointed to the door and said, "Get out of my office, and don't ever come back."

I got out of there as fast as I could and called my mom on the way home. "What the heck am I supposed to do?" I asked her. "I'm trying to change, but I can't get a job, I can't support myself. I don't know what I'm going to do!" As always she was supportive and encouraging, but I had finally realized exactly what my life choices had done. I had made decisions based on the pleasures of the moment—not on my future. And in doing so, I had really messed up my future.

Sober for My Son

Every other time, when I reached this point, I would have gone back to the alcohol or drugs; but the thought of disappointing my son yet again kept me sober. You have to remember, Texas City is a small town, so when I went to jail on crack cocaine and police endangerment charges, it was on the front page of the paper for two days. Everybody in the town knew. When I had tried to help out with my son's Little League team, my past came back and slapped me hard. I was an assistant coach, and the coach asked me take over when he couldn't make it for a game. But just as the game was starting, the Little League president came to the field and told me I wasn't allowed to be at the games because of my record. I had to leave the premises as my son sat and watched.

Even though my son loved baseball, he wanted me to be able to share a sport with him so he switched to soccer. Once again, my past came back to haunt me because, at first, they wouldn't let me get a license to coach. Eventually, however, after a phone interview during which I said that while I wasn't proud of what I had done, I wouldn't change anything if it meant that my son would learn from my mistakes, they gave me a license and I began to coach soccer. But through it all, my son had to go through the pain of other kids saying, "Your dad's a dopehead. Your dad's a druggie. Why isn't your dad in jail?"

The pain of realizing what I had done to my son kept me sober and kept me going—even though I didn't have a clue what I was going to do next.

Look for the Open Door

However, one of the lessons I was learning was that when you are willing and ready, the next door will open. You have to look for it and be prepared to step through it, but a door will always open.

My door opened when a real estate agent friend of mine from the twelve-step meetings suggested that I get a real estate license. Remember I said that one skill I had developed was the ability to manipulate people—but that's the dark side of that particular ability. The bright or positive side is that I was a natural salesman. I decided that instead of using that skill to get what I wanted—like drugs—I'd flip the switch and use that ability to help other people get what they wanted and needed—new homes.

So two friends and I began the twelve-week class. When it was over, we all took the real estate exam. They both passed, but I needed to retake one part. I rescheduled and passed it with no problem, and that's when I started to get super excited. My friends had their licenses, and I was just waiting to get mine. A week went by and nothing. Another week. Nothing. A month went by, and I still didn't have my license. I knew I had passed the tests, so I couldn't figure out what the delay was.

Then one day a letter came in the mail. I was so excited when I ripped it open, but my excitement turned to real despair when I read that they regretted to inform me I was not going to be issued a license because of my background. They said I could appeal the decision if I wanted, however.

Of course I wanted to appeal, so I wrote the letter, following the instructions to a tee. Another month went by, and another letter came saying again that I would not be issued a real estate license due to my background. Once again, the letter said that I could appeal the decision.

By now I was getting fed up. I knew that I had changed and wasn't going to let some clerk somewhere ruin my chances at creating a new and better life, so I set up an in-person interview. As part of the interview process, I was allowed to bring a character witness, so I brought my friend from the twelve-step program who had originally encouraged me to apply for a real estate license.

When we got to the interview, there were video cameras recording everything my friend and I said. A real estate lawyer and judge were there, and they both began drilling me with questions about my life and my decisions. I stayed as calm as I could, even though I was feeling some of those old feelings of being inadequate and unworthy. However, I just kept thinking about my son and the promise I had made to him. That promise meant more to me than anything else ever had.

What Would I Do Differently?

Finally, they asked me one final question: If you could do your life all over again, what would you change? I know they expected me to say I would never have gotten involved with drugs or that I would have taken my first treatment center back in college more seriously. What I said shocked them. I said that I would not change one single thing. I told them that I would live my life exactly the same way I did because if it taught my son how not to live and helped him avoid my mistakes, it was all worth it.

When I walked out of there, I figured I'd never hear from them again. When a month passed, I was sure that they had shredded my application, but I had meant every word—if seeing how I had messed up my life helped my son live a better life, I would do it all over again.

I did need to earn some money, so I got a job at Walmart. My shift was from 3:00 p.m. to 11:00 p.m., unloading trucks. It was hard labor, but it was a job. The first day we didn't get off until about 4:00 a.m. I was beat when I got home, but I kept telling myself that at least I had a job.

Before I went to bed, I looked at my mail and there was my real estate license. I can remember just standing there, staring at that piece of paper like it was the golden ticket to the future. The next day, I thanked Walmart for the job but explained that I was going to go into real estate.

I immediately went to the office where my two friends who had gotten their licenses were working and began to sell real estate with them.

Wanting More

I was good at selling real estate, and it was enough for a while. But though I was doing okay, I had bigger dreams. I wanted more. Yes, I wanted more things like a bigger house and a better car, but I also wanted to create a lifestyle that fulfilled me on a deeper level. I wanted to build a good relationship with my son. I wanted my parents to be proud of me. I wanted to create a positive legacy. But most of all, I wanted to help other people understand that it's never too late to create a new and better life.

That's when I joined Ambit Energy. It is a multi-level marketing company that provides electricity and natural gas services in deregulated energy markets in the United States.

That was also the time when I started to believe that dreams really can come true.

"You gotta have a dream, if you don't have a dream, how you gonna have a dream come true?

— **"Happy Talk"** *from South Pacific*

I allow myself to dream about a better and bigger life. Without a dream, I will never have a dream come true.

Chapter Ten

As I said, my life didn't do an instant 180 when I made that promise to my son. I still had some rocky times, but I was at least moving forward. The biggest problem continued to be figuring out how to make a living. I was selling real estate, but for whatever reason, I just didn't click with real estate. I did well in it, but nothing exceptional. And it just didn't feel like it was the answer I had been looking for, so I opened my mind to new possibilities. That's when I first discovered network marketing.

Hope Rises

A friend introduced me to a direct marketing company dealing with travel, and I joined right away. I didn't succeed in achieving financial freedom through that company, but I began to see potential in myself and to have hope again.

I dabbled in network marketing for several years, but in October of 2006, a red-letter month in my personal history, I didn't have a dime to spare. I mean that literally. I was barely hanging on financially, despite my involvement with the travel company and with real estate sales. A friend invited me to go to Dallas to learn about Ambit Energy, but

I didn't even have enough money for gas for the 250-mile trip, much less money to invest in the startup. I was planning to let this opportunity go, but something made me stop. I put my pride aside and asked a friend if he could take me.

When we got there, I listened to the presentation and all of sudden knew that this was the something I was meant to do. I'll admit I didn't see the whole potential at the time, but I saw that Ambit would allow me to pay my bills on time and that's really all I could envision at the moment. I was thirty-eight years old; I had been through foreclosures, car repossessions, and bankruptcies; and I wasn't making enough money to support myself, much less my son. The thought of being able to pay every bill on time seemed like a dream come true. I didn't even dare to dream beyond that.

I swallowed my pride a second time and asked a friend if she could lend me the startup money. I have to say right now that if she hadn't been willing to loan me that couple of hundred dollars, I wouldn't be where I am today; so thank you, from the bottom of my heart.

At that first meeting, I asked what I had to do to be successful, and the consultant told me, "Make phone calls." I figured I could do that, and I knew that if I didn't do something different with my life, it was going to be just the same—or worse—next year and the year after.

So that night, I went home and started making phone calls. The first two people laughed at me, but the third person listened. And that's how it all began.

The Power of the Mind

At that moment, I truly understood two things: first, nothing is more powerful than the made-up mind; and second, everything happens to us for a reason. After so many years of trying and failing, things finally came together for me. As I look back, I can see that the process started when I was in jail with the million-dollar bonds. I started to become a different person then, but once I found my niche, things really began to change rapidly.

As I began to build my business, I learned two important lessons. The first is that God gave us two ears and one mouth, and I believe the reason is that we are supposed to listen twice as much as we talk! That was a major lesson for me, the guy who always thought he knew everything.

The second big lesson came from the fact that when I got involved with direct marketing, I became involved with positive people who wanted to make a positive difference in the world on an everyday basis. I began to really recognize the Power of the Mind and how what we think affects our entire world. As a result, I learned that what I think creates my world. If I think negative thoughts, I'm going to get negative results. If I think positive thoughts, I'm going to get positive results.

Prior to network marketing, I had been given the opportunity to share my addiction and recovery story through the twelve-step program. I was comfortable enough to be able to tell people that the program was a way out of our destructive lifestyles and that we don't have to use alcohol and drugs; instead, we can try to become somebody. I already had that experience. But network marketing allowed me the opportunity to talk about people's families and finances and future.

I believe that everything happens for a reason. The first network marketing company I joined didn't propel my family to any kind of financial prosperity, but it gave me a chance to learn how to help people. What really made the difference was when I started meeting regularly with my personal Ambit sponsor, Steve Thompson. Every weekend that I didn't have my son, I drove 250 miles to my sponsor's home in Austin to learn what I could. I would get upset if someone else was there because I felt he or she was intruding on my time with him. I would ask questions about network marketing, about leadership, and about life skills. I would just sit and listen. I sat with a pad in hand and hoped it wasn't going to be a sixty-second answer because I wanted to learn everything I could from him. Thanks so much, Steve.

He didn't make a penny off me, but he gave me the chance to change the way I thought. And once I changed the way I thought, I changed my actions. And once I changed my actions, all the things that I had never thought possible suddenly became reality. It all started with my mindset, the Power of the Mind.

These two lessons sound so simple and, in fact, they are. But I had to go through a lot of heartache to finally learn them. I hope that you can learn from my experience and recognize how much your own life can improve once you change the way you think. Your self-esteem, your financial situation, and your relationships can all become better than you ever imagined.

I think Og Mandino summarizes it best in his book, *The Greatest Miracle in the World*:

> Most humans, in varying degrees, are already dead. In one way or another they have lost their dreams, their ambitions, their desire for a better life. They have surrendered their fight for self-esteem, and they have compromised their great potential. They have settled for a life of mediocrity, days of despair and nights of tears. They are no more than living deaths confined to cemeteries of their choice. Yet they need not remain in that state. They can be resurrected from their sorry condition. They can each perform the

greatest miracle in the world. They can each come back from the dead...

And speaking of miracles, it is through network marketing that I experienced my greatest miracle—the discovery of my soul mate, my partner in business and in life. Now I'll let her tell you her part of our story.

> *"All our dreams can come true, if we have the courage to pursue them."*
>
> **— Walt Disney**

Today I choose to have the courage to pursue my dreams and the confidence that they will come true.

Debbie's Story

Chapter Eleven

When I first met Chris, I had already accomplished many of the things people say are important. I had gone to school. I had gotten married. I had two great kids. I was a registered nurse, and I loved helping people. I was making a six-figure income, even though I had to work two jobs to do it. Life was okay. It wasn't great, but it wasn't bad either. I thought that I would just sort of continue down that same road until I retired. After that, well, I didn't really think much beyond that.

All of that changed with Chris. Through him, I learned the importance of having dreams and goals. I learned that just because things have always been one way, that doesn't mean they have to be that way for the rest of our lives.

But most important, I learned from Chris that we all have special characteristics in us that we haven't unleashed yet. It may be because we haven't had the right opportunity, or it may be because we never had anyone who believed in us.

BC and AC

In some ways, I divide my life into two parts: BC and AC—Before Chris and After Chris. I truly believe that all I experienced before meeting him was to help me appreciate what it is truly possible to achieve. In the time I've been with Chris, I've come to understand that when you are so passionate about something that it keeps you awake at night, that's when your special qualities will surface. These are the qualities that will empower you to strive to do a little better every day … that will empower you to set goals that you never thought were possible—and achieve them! And that's when you will find the power to believe in yourself and what you can accomplish, no matter how old you are or what you might have done in your past.

It truly is never too late to live the life of your dreams.

"We become what we think about most of the time, and that's the strangest secret."

— **Earl Nightingale**

I know that I am uniquely created and have a gift to offer the world by my presence.

Chapter Twelve

Like Chris, I'm a Texan, born and bred. I was born in Galveston even though my dad was from Brooklyn and my mother was from Oregon. My mother's dad died when she was very young, so she was put in an orphanage because her mother wasn't able to take care of her and her siblings. Eventually she was adopted by a coach and his wife, and her adoptive parents took family vacations to Texas. One year they visited Galveston, and my mother thought it was the prettiest place she had ever seen. Right then and there, she decided that she loved the tropical setting, the weather, and the Southern lifestyle, and that she would leave the cold Oregon winters and move south when she was old enough. And one day, she did just that. She packed up her bags and headed to Texas.

My dad's family was from Italy—a real old-world family. His mother never learned to speak English—she spoke only Italian to the day she died. They were a very close-knit family, like a lot of Italians, and I think my dad expected to live his entire life in Brooklyn. I know his mom expected that! But, as I've learned, things don't always turn out the way we think—and often that's a good thing.

Galveston

My dad worked at a linen company in New Jersey with a friend, Tony Cuchia, who had married a Galveston girl. Tony kept telling him that if he wanted to see paradise on Earth, he needed to see Galveston. My dad had served in World War II, and after the war ended, he decided that if he had put his life on the line serving this nation, he ought to see more of it. So he began to travel around the country. Of course, he went to Galveston and, just like my mom, he fell in love with the area. It was hard on his mother because he was the first of the family to leave home, and it seemed to her that he was moving to a whole different part of the world; but he just knew that he wanted to live in Texas. I guess he didn't think that Brooklyn was paradise!

The Balinese Room

He moved to Galveston and got a job working in the back room at the Balinese Room. The Balinese was a famous nightclub built in 1929 on a pier stretching from the Galveston Seawall 600 feet out over the waters of the Gulf of Mexico. A lot of stars like Frank Sinatra, Bob Hope, George Burns, and the Marx Brothers performed there. And it was known for running illegal gambling. My dad told me the band used to play "The Eyes of Texas" when the authorities were coming so those in the back room had time to turn over all the gambling tables and make it look like it was just an innocent supper club! It helped that the club was long and narrow. By the time the authorities got to the very back room where the gambling was taking place, all the evidence was gone. Unfortunately, the club was destroyed in 2008 by Hurricane Ike. Only some rubble and its famous red door were left after Ike came through, but it was a real hotspot in my dad's day.

Dad was a go-getter, so he also started working at Hygeia Chemical as a deliveryman. Actually, Hygeia is still around as a distributor of commercial and industrial cleaning supplies and equipment. Dad worked his day job at Hygeia Chemical, then he'd head down the pier and work nights at the Balinese Room.

Now as luck—or fate—would have it, my mom got a job at Hygeia Chemical and a job as a hostess at the Balinese Room at the exact same time that my dad was employed there! I think it must have been a pretty exciting time for the two of them. They worked at two of the same places. What were the odds of that?

As They Say

They started out working together and eventually fell in love and got married. Because they both thought Galveston was as close to paradise as they could get, they decided that's where they wanted to raise their family— and the rest is, as they say, history.

I lived much of my childhood as pretty much an only child because my brother is ten years older and my sister is thirteen years younger. I have no complaints about my childhood. I attended grade school at St. Patrick's Catholic School, then went on to Ball High School. I did all the normal things girls my age did. I played with Barbie dolls and hung out with my friends, and I was a Girl Scout. Galveston is just a great area for being outside; it's right on the water and has terrific weather, so I spent a lot of my childhood outdoors riding my bike and playing kickball. When I was in high school, I was part of the famous Ball High School Tornette Drill Team; one year we even performed at the Dallas Cowboys football game half-time show.

I had the advantage of having parents who loved me and always did their best to give me and my brother and sister everything we needed—even if we didn't get everything we wanted. It's not good for kids to have everything they want handed to them anyway; they never learn to appreciate what they have when that happens.

Even though we grew up in basically the same area, Chris and I didn't know each other because we lived in different towns.

Destined to Be

Our lives just seemed destined to be together. The reason I say this is that I was born one day before Chris's sister. St. Mary's Hospital in Galveston isn't all that big and, in those days, they kept the moms and babies for three days after a birth. That's why I know that, at one point, my dad and Chris's dad were standing there in the nursery together, looking at their baby girls through the window. I don't have any proof, but I know it had to have happened. There were only so many babies in the nursery at that time and visiting hours were limited, so I'm sure my dad and Chris's dad met there. I can just see them standing there at the nursery, looking at their little girls and chatting a bit, never knowing that someday their families would be joined.

Then Chris's mom and dad went back to Texas City and my parents took me home. It was only later that Chris and I realized I had been in the same nursery in the same hospital at the same time as his sister. If that isn't fate, I don't know what is, because Chris is truly my soul mate!

"Love is our true destiny. We do not find the meaning of life by ourselves alone—we find it with another."

— **Thomas Merton**, *Love and Living*

Today I am open to giving and receiving love because I know that love is my true destiny.

Chapter Thirteen

The one thing that is notable about my childhood is that I was very, very, very shy. Talking to people made me so nervous that I just avoided making conversation. The irony of being shy is that people think you are stuck up and that you think you are too good to be with them when, in fact, you are just afraid. I know I got the reputation of being stuck up in high school, when I was just so shy I could hardly stand it. What is so amazing is that in those days I was too afraid to talk to anyone, and now I talk to every stranger I meet! That's just another example of how it's never too late to make a positive change in your life. Had I allowed my shyness to keep controlling me, I would never be where I am today. I would not have the things I have, and I would not be with Chris and our families.

Peaceful Center to Life

One of the best gifts I was given as I grew up and one that actually helped me develop self-confidence despite being so shy was that I had a really great relationship with my parents. Because of that, I always had a kind of peaceful center to my life.

Mom was a stay-at-home mom. She did go to work as a school bus driver after I got older, but for much of my life, she was home with me. Dad's work meant he was gone a lot, but when he was home, he would spend time with me as well. I was very fortunate in that regard.

One of the best memories I have is when Mom started decorating cakes. She really got into cake decorating. She took classes and learned to make absolutely gorgeous wedding cakes as well as cakes for birthdays and other special occasions. Some of her wedding cakes were four feet tall! I remember helping her deliver her cakes when I was just seven years old. I often thought that she was almost like an artist with her cake-decorating talent, and I guess she actually was. It was difficult, and she would spend hours making roses and other detailed decorations to put on these cakes. Everything she made was super detailed, and I was awed by every cake she ever made because they were works of art. She eventually stopped that business and began driving a school bus, but I still remember her gorgeous cakes.

Family Love

My childhood memories are good ones. In fact, one of my best memories is sharing time with my brother. We are ten years apart, but we were and still are very close. When he went into the Marines at age eighteen, I was devastated and wrote to him all the time. After he got out and came back, it was as if no time had elapsed at all. The one thing about my brother is that he has always been able to keep me laughing.

The Importance of Support

One thing about my upbringing that has really influenced me now in my business is the way my mother took such care to give us support and compliments. Being positive and supportive to those you work with is one way that you can ensure not only your own success, but also the success of those around you. I remember my mom sending out Hallmark cards, and she always took the time to write a special message to the recipient. She had a gift for writing exactly what someone needed to hear. I used to tell her she should work for Hallmark because their verses were nothing compared to what she wrote.

Every time I got a birthday card or Christmas card or a card for any event in my life from my mom, it would have a special message in it just for me. But Mom did that for everyone she loved. For example, she would take my sons to have portraits made as they were growing up. On the back of the pictures she would write about them, what they were doing, what they liked, and how much she loved them. They still have those pictures now, and they treasure them. Because I know how much her actions meant to me when I was growing up and to my sons when they were small, I try to always see the good in others and encourage them as much as I can.

Working with Dad

But it wasn't just my mom who helped form me into the person I am today. My dad was a big influence on me as well.

I mentioned that he worked in the back room at the Balinese Club where gambling would take place. At the time, Galveston was pretty liberal about gambling, but eventually the state decided to shut it all down. I heard stories that the Texas Rangers shut down the Balinese Club by just sitting there day after day until there were no more customers. Whatever happened, my dad eventually had to find another job that was legal. A lot of the people he worked with at the club moved to Las Vegas to open up casinos there, but my mother didn't want to move to Las Vegas, so he looked around for something he could do in Galveston.

Since Galveston is right on the Gulf Coast, there is a lot of fishing in the area. He decided to take advantage of that by opening a wholesale fishing tackle business. He got a little white minivan, bought some supplies, and began to make sales. He'd take the profit from the sales and buy some more supplies and do it all over again. Eventually, he ended up selling fishing tackle along the entire Gulf Coast.

He started out selling in Galveston, but when he retired thirty years later, he was buying direct from the big manufacturers and selling tackle everywhere.

While I learned from my mother the importance of recognizing and encouraging others, I learned from my dad the value of repeating the same steps over and over in your business until you are successful. Dad started out small, but he just kept selling, buying more merchandise with his profits, selling that, and buying more. He did it over and over until he eventually built a very successful business. When I got into direct sales with Chris, that lesson really came back to me. I learned from Dad what it took to be successful, and I applied those steps over and over. I didn't try to invent a new way of doing things. I did what others had proven to be successful. But that's something Chris and I will talk about a little later.

"Far and away the best prize that life has to offer is the chance to work hard at work worth doing."

— Teddy Roosevelt

I take the necessary steps to secure my success. With each step I take, I come closer to accomplishing my dreams and goals.

Chapter Fourteen

When I first got out of high school, I attended business college for a year, then I started working at a bank. After about four years at the bank, my dad said he needed some help with his business and asked if I would like to come work with him. He said he would match my bank salary and give me weekends off. That sounded pretty good to me since I was working a half day at the bank every Saturday, so I resigned at the bank and went to work with my dad.

Family Business

Along the way, I got married and had two sons. Working together as a family was a real blessing. I was able to work with my parents and still be with my sons as they were growing up. My sons got to spend time with their grandparents as well. My parents lived in a two-story house. The business was on the first floor, and they lived on the second. Even though my mom was driving a school bus at the time, she was back home by 9:30 a.m., so I could take my babies to work with me, and my mom was there to watch them. I worked on the first floor in what we called the warehouse. Dad went out and made the sales while I filled the orders, maintained the inventory, and did some of the purchasing. I guess I did a little bit of everything, but that's how it is in a family business. It was wonderful because it was a family business, and it really pleases me that we are continuing that family tradition of working together because now both my boys work with me in direct sales. I know from my own life what a great blessing it was to be able to spend time with family.

Of course, we had tough times like any other business owners. When earnings are slim, you pay yourself less and less. And though we were wholesaling for the whole Gulf Coast, it seemed money was usually tight because our business was seasonal. There's not a whole lot of fishing along the Gulf in the dead of winter, so we worked hard to earn enough money in the summer months to make it through that part of the year. That's why Mom drove a school bus and why I frequently worked at part-time jobs in the winter when there wasn't enough money to pay my salary.

Tough Times

My financial situation was really bad once I became a single mom. I have a very vivid memory when my sons were ten and six, and we arrived home one night to find our lights weren't working. So we ate peanut butter and jelly sandwiches for supper and did homework by candlelight. I knew my electricity had been turned off because I couldn't make ends meet, but I told the boys, "Oh my gosh! It must have been a transformer. I saw a truck at the end of the street and it's okay. I'm sure they'll be on tomorrow." I told them the story when they got older, and they remembered the incident, but they didn't have a clue at the time that finances were so tight for us.

In those days, I dreamed about what it would be like to have enough money coming in every month that I didn't have to work. I would think about what it would be like if I could just sit on the floor and play with my kids all day. I would try to imagine what that life would be like. I knew that there were people out there who lived that life, and I used to ask myself, *What do they do that I can do so I don't have to go to work all the time?* While I was in the van making deliveries for our business, that's what I would be dreaming about—how maybe one day something would happen that would allow me to have enough money that I wasn't always scraping by. I would dream about it, but I didn't actually believe the dream could come true. When I finally realized that dreams can come true if you have a plan, set goals, envision the future, and take concrete steps, I was able to have that life.

The Importance of Gratitude

Sometimes I wish I had learned this lesson sooner, but then I tell myself to just be grateful for what I have now without regretting the past.

The past helps shape us, but it's what we do right now, in the present, that determines our lives. And being grateful is an essential part of that. As Rhonda Byrne says in *The Secret*, a book that totally changed my life, "Be grateful for what you have now. As you begin to think about all the things in your life you are grateful for, you will be amazed at the never-ending thoughts that come back to you of more things to be grateful for. You have to make a start, and then the Law of Attraction will receive those grateful thoughts and give you more just like them."

If I were to suggest you do one thing today to make a huge difference in your life, it would be to be grateful for everything—because gratitude changes everything.

"If the only prayer you said was thank you, that would be enough."

— **Meister Eckhart**

I am grateful for every person and everything in my life. I am blessed beyond measure.

Chapter Fifteen

When my dad got a little older and wanted to retire, my sister and I took over the day-to-day operations of the business. But it became too difficult for two women to run a fishing tackle business without bringing in more employees, and we didn't really want to do that; so my dad sold the business, and I found myself unemployed.

Registered Nurse

I had to do something to support my boys and myself, so I went to nursing school in Galveston at the University of Texas Medical Branch. It was in the work/school program that I discovered my love for taking care of pediatric patients, so my first job as an RN was in the pediatric emergency room.

I loved being an ER nurse, but it was very stressful work. Every decision can be a matter of life or death. However, being a nurse gave me a lot of insight into human nature and how people react when they are scared or hurting. At the time I didn't realize it, but all of those experiences were training me to work in direct sales. I learned to hear what people weren't saying as well as what they were saying, if you know what I mean. I learned to watch for subtle body clues, and I learned to ask the right questions. I learned to really pay attention to people, and that's what life is really all about—people.

The Secret in *The Secret*

I know Chris says that he wouldn't change a thing about his life, and while I'm not sure I'd say the same, I do know that I am forever grateful for everything that has happened to me. To quote *The Secret* again, "A lot of people feel like they're victims in life, and they'll often point to past events, perhaps growing up with an abusive parent or in a dysfunctional family. Most psychologists believe that about eighty-five percent of families are dysfunctional, so all of a sudden you're not so unique … The real question is, what are you going to do now? What do you choose now? Because you can either keep focusing on that, or you can focus on what you want. And when people start focusing on what they want, what they don't want falls away and what they want expands, and the other part disappears.

Lessons from a Baseball Glove

I often remind myself to remember the past. Not to go back and dwell on it, but to remember it so that I can be grateful for the present. One memory that keeps me striving to do better every day has to do with my oldest son, Bobby. We were on our way to his Little League game when his baseball glove ripped. It was a little old cheap K-

Mart glove, and I knew he wasn't going to be able to use that glove, so I went to the sporting goods store. Remember that Galveston was a small town, so there was only one place that sold sporting goods at that time. We went into the store, and I said to the owner, "Archie, I've got to get a glove for Bobby. We're on our way to the game, and his glove just ripped." He replied, "Son, go back there and pick you out one." So my son went back and picked out this beautiful glove. I think it was made of kangaroo skin. He was so excited when he came up to us and said, "This is it! This is it! I'll never need another glove!" Archie agreed that it was a wonderful glove. It was the best glove I'd ever seen. Then I looked at the price tag. It was $110. I couldn't believe that a glove could cost that much money. Remember, the one he had was a cheap one. I looked at the glove, then I looked at Archie. I'm sure he could tell by the shocked look on my face that I was going to have to tell my son there was no way I could buy that glove. Archie paused for a minute, then said, "Take the glove, and pay me five dollars a week."

Still today, I get tears in my eyes when I think about what Archie did for us that day. I thanked him, and every single week I was in there paying $5 until I paid it off. Bobby knows that story now, but he had no idea how tight things were at the time. And today, the fact that I can say we have enough financial freedom that I could buy a $110 glove without thinking about it is just amazing.

Control Your Thoughts

During my days as a single mom trying to pay the bills, I didn't really believe life could change so much. Therefore, when I tell you that it's never too late, I hope you take it to heart. It all begins with what you think and what you believe. So I would encourage you to start thinking about what you want—not what you don't want! I would urge you to begin controlling every thought and being focused on the good that awaits you, because, as the Law of Attraction (which I believe with all my heart) says, "What you think about comes about."

"See the things that you want as already yours."

— Rhonda Byrne, *The Secret*

Today I will concentrate on that which is good, beautiful, loving, kind, and affirming. Negative thinking has no place in my life.

Chapter Sixteen

In order to get ahead financially, I started working two full-time jobs. I was offered a position as a school nurse, so during the day I worked with the kids, and then right after school ended, I went to my second job as a specialist at the Poison Control Center. I worked from 7:00 a.m. to 1:30 a.m. the next morning. Sometimes it was dark when I went to work and dark when I got off to go home! I'd go outside during my work breaks just to see the sunlight!

The Power of Positive Thinking

It was right about then that things began to change dramatically. I know I keep talking about *The Secret*, but that book has played such an important part in my life that I want people to understand its power. When I was younger, I had read *The Power of Positive Thinking* by Norman Vincent Peale. For those of you who don't know about him, Peale was one of the first people to talk about how the power of our thoughts can transform our lives. Anyway, I read his book and remember thinking that it made a lot of sense; but there wasn't anyone for me to talk to about it. When I mentioned it to my dad, he sort of dismissed the whole notion, so I just put it in the back of my mind. Years later when I found *The Secret*, it validated everything I had read before. Everything really does begin with your thoughts, so when you change your thoughts, you change your world. I was introduced to network marketing while working those two full-time jobs, and that's when my life really began to change.

Network Marketing

To tell the truth, I wasn't all that excited about network marketing at first. A girlfriend had joined a travel network marketing company and wanted me to join too. I told her that I already had two full-time jobs and had neither the time nor the energy for another job. Then she said, "Debbie, every time you take a vacation, you can make money off of it." I still wasn't interested. I told her, "Look, you know what? You book our vacations and you make the money. Just leave me out of it." So she did. She and I went on two great vacations that year—one to Las Vegas and another to New York—but I still wasn't interested in joining network marketing.

We got back from our New York trip and she called me a few weeks later. "Hey, I'm having fajitas on Friday night," she said. "You want to come over?" Well, it happened that was one night I didn't have to work, so I agreed. It sounded like it would be a nice, relaxing evening.

Feeling Snookered

As soon as I walked through the front door, I realized that we weren't just having dinner. A bunch of people who I had never seen before were there and a projector and screen were set up at the front of the room. *Uh oh*, I thought to myself, *I don't think I want to be here.* That's when it dawned on me that there was going to be some kind of presentation, and I suspected it was going to be about the travel business. *No way am I going to get involved in that*, I thought. *I'm out of here.* I turned around and headed for the door, but my friend spotted me and insisted I at least have a fajita before I left. I reluctantly obliged.

A bit later she introduced me to Chris and said he was the one who was going to make the presentation. I remember thinking that all I wanted to do was get out of there, but I was stuck. Keep in mind, though, that I was born and raised in the South and Southern ladies are just that—ladies. So I didn't say anything about feeling snookered, although I'm sure it must have shown on my face.

Chris gave his presentation, but I was still thinking about how fast I could get out of there. He came up to me afterward and asked if I was interested. I told him I was already working two jobs and didn't have the time or energy to work another one. I also shared that I was trying to put aside enough money to retire, so spending money on travel wasn't a priority right then.

The next day I decided to join, but I didn't do much with it because I didn't have the time to put into the business. However, even though I didn't know it at the time, that fajita night was the start of an entirely new life for me. I didn't recognize it, but I was being shown the door to fulfilling my dreams—including finding my soul mate.

"You can't connect the dots looking forward; you can only connect them looking backward. So you have to trust that the dots will somehow connect in your future. You have to trust in something—your gut, destiny, life, karma, whatever. This approach has never let me down, and it has made all the difference in my life."

— Steve Jobs

I trust that my future is unfolding exactly as it should.

Chapter Seventeen

I was making a six-figure annual income at this time, but I was also working about sixty hours a week. So, Chris Atkinson and network marketing were about the last things on my mind. Then, about three weeks after the fajita fiasco, I got another call from my friend. This time she didn't offer me fajitas but said, "You told me that you wanted to make enough money to retire. Well, I think I found something for you." Chris had learned about Ambit and called to offer her the opportunity. Since she was already involved in another energy network marketing company, she turned him down but gave him my number. She was calling to warn me that he would be contacting me.

I had no sooner said that I didn't want any part of it when my caller ID showed Chris was on the line. I remember feeling a bit frustrated with my friend, but I took Chris's call.

He had told me only a little about the company before I interrupted to say in no uncertain terms that I wasn't interested. He responded by saying, "You don't even know what you aren't interested in!"

When "No" Doesn't Mean "No"

I had to admit that was true, so I told him that if he was willing to drive to Galveston, which was about thirty-five miles from his place, I'd give him exactly fifteen minutes of my time. I let him know this was my first weekend off in twenty-one straight days, and I wasn't going to waste a minute of it. In fact, I told him that I would tell him no in person, even if he did come. I figured he would refuse, but to my surprise, he agreed.

When he showed me the outline, I began to get interested. I could see the potential and the possibility, but I was cautious. "Do you think this will work?" I asked.

Chris was honest and said that he didn't know for sure, but he was willing to take a chance on it. I took a deep breath and signed up that night. I call it my Pool Weekend, because that's what I did the rest of the weekend. I relaxed in my pool and thought about what I had just done. I was excited to see if it would work, and I finally felt some hope for my financial future and time freedom.

On Monday I went to work at 7:00 a.m. as usual. By about 10:00 a.m., I was so stressed and overwhelmed that I called Chris and told him I didn't know what I had been thinking when I agreed to join the company, I had too much to do already, and joining would be just too much. I said I didn't know where to start or what to do, and I was overwhelmed.

One More Chance

Well, one thing about Chris is that he is persistent. He invited me to attend a training session in Dallas in a couple of weeks and said if I still wanted to quit after that, he would give me back my startup money. I took him at his word and agreed to go—having no idea at the time that he was broke!

During the training, I learned exactly what I would have to do to make this opportunity work and thought, *I can do that.* I began to see that I could buy back my time, not work as many hours, and have what I had always dreamed of—time freedom. But to have time freedom, you must first have financial freedom. The more I looked at the business, the more I realized that it really was possible to have the life of my dreams.

I started working in ten- to fifteen-minute blocks. On my breaks, during my lunch hour, anytime I had a few minutes, I would make a couple of calls. Slowly but surely the ball began to roll and, within six months, I was making a pretty decent side income.

Following My Dream

I was becoming more and more involved with Ambit and the money was starting to come in, so I retired from my night job. Instead of working nights and weekends, I was going to Ambit meetings and making calls. By now I

109

realized how profitable the business was going to be. After just six months, I had already replaced more than half of my income—and I knew what I had to do. I just couldn't face going back to the sixty-hour weeks and all the stress that accompanied that life.

My sons were grown and lived in Austin, and I was no longer married, so I was free to make the move. I dove into the business, and that's pretty much all I did for a while. I went to training meetings, built my team, called people, and focused my thoughts and goals on the kind of future I wanted to have.

I made some sacrifices, but I could see the bigger picture. I could see that the work I was investing was going to pay off so that I could finally have the time and financial freedom I had always dreamed about—and have it in the not-too-distant future.

"If you don't design your own life plan, chances are you'll fall into someone else's plan. And guess what they have planned for you? Not much."

— Jim Rohn

I choose my own path while allowing others to choose theirs. I accept everyone as they are, but I continue to pursue my own dream.

Chapter Eighteen

Because Chris sponsored me with Ambit, we had an ongoing business relationship. As I was focusing on building my business, I began to consult him more often. He was building his business at the same time, so we would talk about what worked and what didn't work, and encourage each other to keep going when we were tempted to get discouraged. Somewhere in there, Chris realized that I am pretty direction challenged. I always get lost. Heck, I could even get lost on the small island that I lived on! All of the business meetings were in Houston where driving is crazy, so we started traveling there together.

At the beginning, our relationship was strictly business. I liked Chris as a person, but there wasn't anything romantic about it. I actually assumed he was a confirmed bachelor because he had been divorced for so many years—at least fourteen. So we traveled to meetings together and talked business. It was a comfortable relationship, and Chris was always the perfect gentleman.

A "Wow" Moment

Then one day after about eighteen months, he leaned over and kissed me out of the blue. I responded by saying, "Wow. What brought that on?" He replied, "Well, I've just kind of been building up to that." I was really surprised, but I'll admit I was pleased too.

We began to date—we actually went places that weren't work related! At first there wasn't any commitment, but gradually, we began to spend more and more time together and realized we really enjoyed each other's company. Our relationship was already very good because we had spent so much time together in the business. We had grown to really respect each other and had, in fact, become best friends. One thing led to another, and we moved into a house on Clear Lake on July 1, 2008, so we could be together full time.

I think because of the time we had already spent together as friends and coworkers, and because we saw how easily we fit together, it was easy for us to move our relationship along pretty quickly. Since we had spent nearly a year and a half just being good friends, it wasn't like we were two strangers rushing into a commitment. When we realized we were getting serious, we wanted to see if we could make it as a couple.

A Big Surprise

Chris has a bit of an old-fashioned romantic streak in him. While I was okay with the way things were, he wanted to make our commitment more public. The first weekend in September was our company's conference, called Ambition. It's an annual event put on by the corporate office, and all the consultants get together to recognize high achievers and encourage each other. The conference includes multiple events where people are on stage talking about various aspects of the business. Attendees receive training from the corporate office as well as other top Ambit leaders, then corporate makes announcements about where the company is headed next. It's like a company Christmas party because they give away so many awards to the top achievers—things like Cadillacs and motorcycles. It's really an amazing event that I look forward to every year.

Chris had decided to propose to me during that year's Ambition conference. However, he didn't tell me about his plans. He arranged everything with the corporate office and told a bunch of consultants that he was going to propose to me on stage. It just amazes me that so many Ambit consultants could keep it a secret, because in our business we are always spreading the word and talking to as many people as possible. But Chris told them all that it was a secret and not to breathe a word—and I honestly didn't have a clue that anything out of the ordinary was going to happen.

The Saturday night gala event is a very formal affair that includes dinner with presentations, then a dance. I got all dressed up and was excited to be seeing friends and being part of this huge, fancy affair.

Chapter Eighteen

The corporate office, including the cofounders and many national consultants, was in on the secret—which was key to Chris's plan. During the presentations, the corporate executives announced that they were going to bring a few people on stage to talk about a new program the company was offering. They selected three people from around the room, and Chris was the fourth. I remember thinking, "This is cool! Chris just got picked to be part of this new program presentation." I still didn't have the foggiest idea this was all part of the surprise he had planned for me.

Esther Spina, a friend and national consultant, got up and spoke very briefly about the new program, but that didn't seem odd to me. Then, holding the microphone, she walked over to the next person and asked a few questions and did the same for the next person. But when she moved on to Chris, she handed him the mic and walked off the stage.

At the time I thought that was sort of odd, but still nothing registered. I just assumed that Chris had some new information to share. It was one of those "that's kind of weird" moments, but I didn't have too long to wonder about it because the next thing I heard was Chris saying, "I can't do a testimony without my partner up here," and he motioned for me to join him on the stage.

By the Book

I got up and moved toward him, but all the time I was thinking, *I'm not the one picked to give the testimonial. We are going to get in so much trouble from corporate because he's not doing what corporate wanted him to do. They asked him to give the testimonial, and now he's bringing me up, and it's not going to be good. He's changing the whole program, and we are both going be in so much trouble!*

You see, all those years of nursing had taught me to do things "by the book," and I wasn't one to bend the rules. I think it's because when you work in the ER and in poison control, you have to be so careful about everything. So I would never have just up and changed things on the spur of the moment.

I remember my heart pounding as I walked toward the stage. I kept thinking, *Oh, Chris, don't do this!* When I got up there, he started talking about how he couldn't do anything without me and didn't want to even give a testimonial without me. I was standing there, looking out at the audience and feeling like I could hardly breathe. I was just terrified that we were going to get in trouble with the corporate office. I didn't know what they would do and didn't want to find out, so I just kept staring straight ahead.

Then I saw out of the corner of my eye that Chris was down on one knee. It was sort of like a dream as I heard him start to propose. My only thought was, *Oh my goodness!* In the pictures they took of me as he proposed, I just look totally dazed—probably because I was!

Put a Ring on It

I remember Chris asking if I would marry him, holding out my hand as he put the ring on my finger, then him standing up for a hug. But I was still thinking that we were going to get in big trouble for having interrupted the program, so I grabbed the microphone and tried to get back to the testimonial. I still hadn't realized it was all staged, so I babbled on about the program for a few seconds, then returned the mic to Chris.

All of a sudden, when everyone began rushing the stage and clapping, it dawned on me that everyone had been in on the secret but me! Chris explained, "Debbie, we weren't really doing a testimonial. That was all set-up to get you up on the stage." I told him I had been totally freaked out because I thought we were going to get in trouble with corporate. To this day, I don't know how everyone could keep a secret like that. It was awesome. And that's how we got engaged and became an official couple!

"There is never a time or place for true love. It happens accidentally, in a heartbeat, in a single flashing, throbbing moment."

— **Sarah Dessen,** The Truth About Forever

Today I choose to be a positive influence on everyone I meet. I know that I am loved, and therefore I can love in turn.

Chapter Nineteen

I sometimes joke that I felt like a hurricane hit when Chris proposed, because a hurricane really *did* hit the day he proposed at that Ambit Ambition conference.

Hurricane Ike

When we left our home for the conference on Tuesday of that week, Hurricane Ike was headed toward Corpus Christi, which is far enough from Galveston that we shouldn't have gotten much more than a little bit of rain. But while we were at the conference, we learned that the storm was moving steadily north until it was heading right to Galveston.

Ike was an enormous storm—a category 4. It was the third most costly of any Atlantic-formed storm and the most costly hurricane to hit Cuba and Texas with the figures running to something like $35 billion in damages. And it was huge. I remember the weather reports saying that Ike was over 600 miles in diameter.

Remember, Chris and I had moved into a house on Clear Lake, which essentially connects to Galveston Bay. The lake should have been safe because it is about a twenty-five minute drive up the channel. But Ike was such an intense storm that it pushed a huge tidal surge clean into Clear Lake. Our house was filled with five feet of water, although we didn't know it at the time.

Losses

We were unable to get home for several days due to debris-covered roads. Even large yachts had broken loose from their berths and were stranded all along the highways. After the hurricane, we had to go to my son's house in Austin and wait it out.

Once the highways were cleared, people were allowed to return to their homes. Since our house was about fifteen feet above sea level, no one expected that area to flood, even in the event of a tidal surge. But the surge from Ike was twenty feet high, so everything on the ground was covered in five feet of water. When we finally reached our house, we found we had lost our cars, including my Trans-Am and Chris's Corvette. In addition, our house was a mess. We had just started moving in a couple of months before, so we had around ninety boxes in the garage that were destroyed. Those boxes included things from my parents, pictures of my kids and family, mementos, and keepsakes—and they were all under water. Our living quarters were on the second level, so what we had there was safe; but all the things we hadn't unpacked were lost forever.

At that point, we spent each day at our house going through the boxes and the mud, trying to clean up what we felt we could salvage and getting rid of the rest. Our area still had no electricity, so the county had enacted a curfew requiring everyone to be off the streets by dark because of the crime and looting. So each evening we'd head to Chris's parents' house in Texas City in order to be inside before curfew. We'd spend the night there and return the next morning to start all over again.

Let's Get Married

Ike came through in the middle of September. It was a huge mess, and I was pretty stressed by it all. In October, after we had been cleaning for a couple of weeks, Chris told me that he wanted to get married on New Year's Eve. I replied, "Okay, next year will be great." Then he said, "No, I mean this year."

I remember standing there in the middle of the mess from Ike, thinking, *You've got to be crazy. There is no way I can plan a wedding for this New Year's Eve.* So I told him, "No, that's not possible. Not this year."

I think I mentioned that Chris can be very persistent ...

He again said, "I want to get married *this* New Year's Eve."

So I said, "If you want to get married this New Year's Eve, then you plan the wedding." I figured with all the devastation from the hurricane, it wasn't going to be possible, but he responded, "Okay, I will."

A little later, I heard him on the phone trying to find a place for us to get married. Every place he called had so much damage they couldn't do a wedding, and I was thinking to myself, *See? Told you so.* Then a little bit later he walked in and said, "Okay, I found a place where we can get married." I asked him where, and he said he'd take me to it. I said, "Okay, this isn't going to work, but I'll go." Kind of reminds you of the day he came to tell me about Ambit, doesn't it? I thought I had my mind made up—but it was before I knew all of the details.

Chris took me to the place, and I was stunned to see a luxurious hundred-foot charter yacht that is used for corporate events, parties, and, yes, weddings! It was amazing. We could have the wedding of our dreams, complete with every detail from the cake to the dinner, on this beautiful boat. As an extra bonus, we could say our vows as we were cruising into the sunset. I never even knew such a thing existed.

But you haven't heard the best part yet. My company is called Princess Energy. I have all this material saying I'm the princess. When I learned that Chris had found a yacht called the *Royal Princess* for our wedding, it convinced me that our marriage was just meant to be. What could I say but, "Wow! Okay, let's do it."

We got married on New Year's Eve in 2008. He took care of all the details, and all I had to do was get my hair and nails done, pick out a dress, and step on board with my flowers. It was magical. I truly felt like a princess at that moment. It was as if I had waited my whole life for this moment.

Life Partners

From that moment on, it hasn't been Chris and Debbie. It's ChrisandDebbie. We truly are partners in all that we do—in our business and our lives. We have developed our philosophy of life that has helped us get where we are today. We want to share it with you in the hopes that, in this next year, all of your dreams can come true as well.

"Being deeply loved by someone gives you strength, while loving someone deeply gives you courage."

— Lao Tzu

I focus on being grateful every day. I look forward to tomorrow, but I live for today.

Creating Your New Life

We aren't special. We haven't been given gifts that no one else in life can have. We aren't better than anybody else in our organization or our lives. We are all equal. We are all put here for some reason. We all have things we want to accomplish.

We firmly believe that to be a real success, you have to want more for other people as well as want more for yourself. Personally, we aren't going to be content or feel like we've reached the pinnacle of our lives until we have helped as many people achieve their goals as we can.

What has allowed us to achieve the things we have achieved is that we have used what we have learned not just for our own benefit, but to help others achieve their goals too.

We want to share some of these lessons with you now. We hope that you can use them to create the life of your dreams because *It's Never Too Late!*

Chapter Twenty:

Dreams

Remember when you were a little kid? You dreamed all the time. You may have dreamed about what you wanted to be when you grew up or what you wanted Santa to bring you at Christmas. You may have pretended that you were a pirate or a princess. Nobody had to teach you to dream. Your imagination was an everyday part of your life. However, as we grow up, we sometimes forget how to dream.

Howard Ikemoto, an artist and art professor, once said, "When my daughter was seven years old, she asked me one day what I did at work. I told her I worked at the college—my job was to teach people how to draw. She stared at me, incredulous, and said, 'You mean they forget?'"

The same is true for dreams ... we forget how to dream.

Forgetting the Power of Dreams

Not only do we forget how to dream, but we also forget the power of our dreams. We begin to forget what it was like to wake up in the morning, excited about the day. We begin to settle for the average, the everyday, the ordinary.

We stop seeing the world as filled with hope and potential. It's as if we put on sunglasses and turn off the lights, then wonder why the world is so dark.

The reasons why we stop dreaming aren't all that hard to understand. Sometimes we don't dream because of the lessons we learned from our parents. Many of us have parents who unintentionally taught us to stop dreaming. They didn't mean to do it, but it happened anyway. For example, many people believe that the only way to get ahead is to go to college, get a good job that pays well, and stick with that until it is time to retire. That might have worked years ago, but it doesn't work anymore. All you have to do is think back a few years to the Great Recession of 2008 when people lost everything they had when the stock market dropped. That time might not go down in history like the Great Depression of 1929, but it still destroyed a lot of lives. People in their seventies were flat broke and trying to live on $1200 a month from Social Security. That was what happened with Chris's parents. They thought they had done things the "right way," but someone changed the "right way" when they weren't looking.

An old adage says a man called to ask if Bob was coming to work that day and his wife replied that Bob was in his casket. He had worked himself to death! Only that's not always a joke nowadays. Too many people are limited because all they dream of is finding a good job and sticking with it until retirement. Then when they retire, they believe they will finally have free time. But that dream has long since disappeared and isn't going to come back any time soon. If you had that as your primary dream, it's no wonder you have stopped dreaming.

Sometimes people stop dreaming simply because they settle for "good enough." They decide that their lives are "good enough" as they are and there isn't any point in trying to improve. Usually these people have stopped dreaming because they allow their lives to be dictated by their current income. Yes, you need to learn how to manage money and live within a budget, but all too often people let their current situation dictate the extent of their dreams. If they can't afford something today, they assume they never will be able to afford it, so they stop dreaming about it.

Another reason we stop dreaming is that we let the analytical, "realistic" side of life take over. When you ask a five-year-old what she wants to be and she says, "A firefighter," you don't immediately ask her if she has the physical ability to pass the tests or if she will become an EMT too or what courses she will take in school. You don't ask her if being a firefighter will give her a pension or ask her what would happen if she got injured on the job. You don't insist that she explain how she would juggle motherhood and firefighting. You don't analyze every aspect of a firefighter's life and try to get her to decide if she has what it takes. You don't dismiss her dream because you can't see how it will be accomplished. No, you just listen to her dream without asking her to set out the exact path she will follow to accomplish that dream.

As adults, we tend to dismiss our dreams because we don't immediately see how we can make them a reality. If you have a dream to own a boat and you don't live near any water, you may immediately decide there isn't any point to having that dream. But dreams don't rely on our normal patterns of reality. We don't have to know all the steps to accomplishment before we begin to dream. The fact is, the dream comes first and then the "how" will open up. We have to be willing to have the dream before we can ever have a dream come true.

Find a Way to Dream Again

If you want to change your life, you must find a way to dream again. It's just that simple. You must allow yourself to dream like you did when you were a child. You must allow yourself to be open to possibilities, hopes, and ideas.

The day you stop dreaming is the day you start dying.

You might be saying to yourself, *That's all well and good, but how do I go about dreaming?* We will get to that soon enough, but for now, just think about what a dream is.

Your Deepest Desires

A dream is nothing more than a way of allowing yourself to recognize your own deepest desires. Everyone has desires. They might be buried so deep that you don't think you can ever recover them, but trust us. Once you make room for a dream in your life, it will rush to the surface and bring a whole lot of other dreams that you've forgotten along with it.

Now we are going to say something that might be a bit controversial, but we believe that the first dream for most people will be for a better life in the form of a bigger house, a better car, a nicer vacation. And that also means more money.

The Reality Behind Dreams

People might claim that their dreams are bigger and loftier than just wanting more money, but when you get honest with them, they will realize that every dream takes money. The hard, cold fact is that whatever your dream is, it is going to take money to finance it.

This is easy to see if your dream is to have a big house on the lake, but think about someone who wants to help the homeless or start a halfway house or create a no-kill facility for animals. We know people who have these as dreams, but none of those dreams can become a reality without funds.

It takes money from somewhere to build that animal shelter or sponsor the homeless or help the addict get off the streets. If someone had never had a dream for a no-kill animal facility, then it probably would never have gotten started. But it took someone with money to provide the building, get the required licensing, hire a staff, and everything else that goes along with it. It's true that a lot of money can come from donations, but in order to be able to donate, you have to have the money to donate. As they say, there is no free lunch.

So we believe that even the most noble dreams have to start with wanting more—and that includes more money.

The Importance of Helping Others

Now here's where the difference comes in. If your dream of having more is just for you, it's probably going to be hard, if not impossible, to achieve. You have to want more for other people as well as for yourself. Your dreams have to be big enough to include the good of other people.

134

Our dream of making a lot of money in our business means we help others make a lot of money as well. We couldn't personally sponsor enough people in our business to buy a brand-new Corvette, but we could grow a business of helping others reach their goals so that we could buy one every month if we wanted.

The most important part of learning to dream is learning to dream big. And that means seeing beyond the circumstances of the moment. It means asking yourself, *What would my life be like if ...?*

But most of all, it means thinking about how you can help other people achieve their dreams, because as you help others achieve their dreams, you can't help but achieve your own as well.

How to Dream

So how do you learn to dream again?

One way is to think back about what you were like as a child, what you loved to do, what made your eyes light up with excitement.

For Chris, it was sports. He loved sports and being outdoors, so when he looked back and thought about it, he realized that many of his adult dreams were going to be centered on sports and sporting activities, like having a jet ski and a sports car.

135

For Debbie, one of her fondest memories was watching her mother bake cakes, so one of her dreams was to have a really great kitchen. She also loved being outdoors and riding her bike, so her dreams included having a pool where she could spend time outdoors enjoying the Texas sunshine.

The best way to learn to dream, however, is to just set aside an afternoon and let your mind wander. Walk outside or through the mall. Pay attention to what catches your eye and ask yourself, *What do I like about that?* Allow yourself to look, to touch, to experience. But in the end, the only real way to learn how to dream again is to give yourself permission to, in the words of Nike, "Just do it!"

"If you take responsibility for yourself, you will develop a hunger to accomplish your dreams."

— Les Brown

Today I will allow myself to dream. I will remember what I loved to do as a child, and I will recapture my lost dreams.

Chapter Twenty-One:

Vision Boards

The first step to a changed life is learning to dream again. But we know that a lot of people have buried their dreams so deeply that they don't even know how to begin.

That's where a Vision Board comes in.

Tangible Picture of Dreams

A Vision Board is simply a physical, tangible picture of your dreams that you can see every single day. It's a way for you to "see" your dreams in real time. It's one of the best ways we know to help you visualize what you want out of life—to put some "skin" on your wishes so that you can eventually turn those wishes into goals.

There's nothing complicated about a Vision Board. Basically, it is any kind of board (paper, wood, cardboard, plastic) on which you put images that represent what you want to have, what you want to do, where you want to go, and what you want to accomplish in your life.

It's a tool that we use to help you not only figure out what your dreams are, but also focus and concentrate on those dreams in a concrete way so that instead of just being someday wishes, they can become concrete goals. (And speaking of goals, we are going to talk about those in the next chapter!)

A Vision Board serves three important purposes. First, it clarifies your dreams. Second, it reinforces those dreams by making them visible. Third, it focuses your mind on those dreams on a daily basis.

Creating a Vision Board

So how do you create a Vision Board?

The first thing to do is ask yourself what it is that drives you crazy at night? What is it that keeps you awake or wakes you up in the middle of the night? What has you saying, "I really want to have X" or "I really want to accomplish Y"? What are some of the bucket-list places that you want to visit before you die? What are those things that just drive you crazy when you see someone else has them or when you hear somebody else talking about them? What grabs your mind and makes you think, *That's truly something I desire more than anything else in the world*? What are those things, ideas, and hopes that make your heart race?

Your Dreams

Just in case you didn't realize it, those are your dreams.

You may have dreamed of ...

- going to Paris
- seeing the Australian outback
- having a house on the beach
- wearing a diamond tennis bracelet
- owning a pair of Jimmie Choo shoes
- buying a Louis Vuitton handbag
- sponsoring an orphan at school
- volunteering with Doctors Without Borders
- planting an English garden
- having a speedboat
- owning a Great Dane
- taking a cruise to Alaska

It doesn't really matter what it is, because everyone is different. No two people have the same dreams, not even you and your spouse. Your dreams are as individual as your fingerprints. All that matters is that a dream is something that awakens a desire in you—a desire that has just been waiting for you to remember it.

Dream Images

The next step is to find images that match your dreams. You can use magazines and cut out pictures or print out images that you find online. It doesn't really matter where they come from, so long as they represent your dreams.

You can get fancy with creating the Vision Board, but we like to keep it simple. Our personal Vision Board is a fifty-cent piece of white poster board from Walmart. We cut out pictures and glue or tape them to the board. It's just like making a kid's collage.

So gather up a whole bunch of pictures and arrange them on the board however you like. There's no science to it. Just have fun. Be a kid again. There's no right or wrong to it. Put whatever stirs your heart and imagination on your Vision Board. On Chris's first Vision Board that he created before we got married, he had a picture of a soccer ball. His son was playing on five soccer teams at the time, and Chris didn't have a soccer ball for his son to practice with—so he wanted to get a ball for him. That first board also had a button-down long-sleeved dress shirt and a sport coat because, at the time, all Chris had was a few T-shirts, a couple of pairs of blue jeans, and a pair of tennis shoes.

On her first board, Debbie had a copy of her first residual check for $12. She made a copy of it and changed the amount to $12,000. One of the reasons was that Chris Chambless, one of the founders of Ambit, always says, "Every magnificent cathedral ever built started with one brick." He assured Debbie that her $12 would be $12,000 in no time. (And in less than a year, it was more than that!)

Big and Little Dreams

After we got married, we created a joint Vision Board. Over the years, the things on our board began to evolve and change. From soccer balls and a sports coat, we began to dream about a house on a lake, family ski vacations, and a gourmet kitchen. However, we started with simple things—things that we believed in our hearts we could obtain. While we really encourage people to put the big dreams on their Vision Board, we also suggest having a few things that aren't so big that you don't begin to doubt your dreams can ever come true. It's important to have both the BIG dreams and smaller, more easily obtainable ones. We use the smaller dreams as stepping stones. Your ultimate goals need stepping stones to encourage you along the way.

Let's say, for example, that you want to clean out the garage. You open the door and stand there, overwhelmed by the mess. You don't see how you will ever be able to get it in order. So you break up the job into little pieces. First you clean the back right corner, then you tackle the side wall. Using that method, bit by bit, you will get that garage clean. That's what we mean by stepping stones. Some dreams are little actions you take that will bring you all the way to your ultimate goal. Rome wasn't built in a day after all!

As you put your pictures on your Vision Board, ask yourself these things: What are some accomplishments I can reach that will show me some positive movement toward my ultimate goal? What can I do to help establish a positive mindset that will enable me to reach my ultimate goal? What are some things that I'd like to have or do that I know are almost within my grasp?

Maybe the things you do could be as simple as getting a new type of gourmet coffee or having the carpets cleaned. Absolutely put those on your Vision Board along with the trip to Paris, because no dream is too big … or too small … if it's something you truly desire.

This Is Why …

Another essential component of your Vision Board is positive, uplifting statements. These can be in the form of goals, such as "I want to have a sprinkler system put in the yard by June 1" or "I want to spend my next birthday in Mexico." They can also be affirming statements such as "I deserve," "I am worthy," or "I am loved." The idea is to stimulate all parts of your imagination so that you can really believe that your dreams will manifest.

Finally, write something like this at the top of your Vision Board: *This is why I do something every day for my business*. It doesn't have to say that it is specifically for your business. You can modify it to fit your own life. You might write, *This is why I do something every day for … my family*, *my career, my health*—whatever motivates you to create a better and more fulfilling life.

Creating a Greater Vision

One question we are sometimes asked is, "Is the purpose of a Vision Board just to acquire material goods?" Of course, the ultimate goal of life isn't just to have more things, but as we said before, Vision Boards are intended to give you concrete images of your dreams. That's why the majority of people start their Vision Boards with the house, the car, the boats, and the vacations.

Really, it all has to do with goals, which we will discuss in the next chapter, but basically, when you actually get that new Corvette and see it sitting in the driveway (or whatever it is you have on your Vision Board), it gives you the confidence and the enthusiasm to keep dreaming because you have physical evidence of a dream that has come true. If you put something intangible like "world peace" on your Vision Board, it would be impossible to measure.

But in the end, your dreams are limitless and can be whatever you want them to be. We've found that as people create Vision Boards and see the results, they often begin to develop dreams and goals that aren't so materially oriented. For example, in our business, someone might have on their Vision Board, *I want more team leaders in my organization.* Or they might write, *I want to be able to give a speech in front of a thousand people without being nervous.* Any of these kinds of things can be dreams.

Our only limitation is ourselves. So dream big!

Displaying Your Vision Board

The last and most important step is to find a place to display your Vision Board. We can't stress enough that you must put it where you will see it often.

A Vision Board has to be placed somewhere prominent in your home. You can't put it in a closet or hide it in the back room. You have to put it where you will see it multiple times a day. It's got to be up for all to see.

Our current Vision Board is taped to the front window of the house in Debbie's office. When we have parties at our house, people come up to us and say, "Okay, where's that room that has your Vision Board? I want to go take a picture."

Some people like to take a picture of their board with their cell phone so they always have it with them. If that works for you, go ahead! Do whatever it takes to keep your Vision Board in front of you multiple times a day.

When you've achieved something on your board, check it off. We like to keep it simple. We take a big black

Sharpie and put a check mark on it. There's nothing like seeing all those check marks to encourage us.

Renew Your Vision

Another question we are asked is how often a person should make a Vision Board. That's really up to you, but we have done five in eight years. We do one when we have achieved most of the things on our current board or when something major has changed in our lives and we want to refocus. A good rule is that if you've looked at your board so often it's become part of the room décor, it's probably time to switch it up with a new Vision Board.

Now, go start picturing your dreams.

"Everything you can imagine is real."

— **Pablo Picasso**

Today I create an image of the future I want to have. I believe that my dreams can become my reality.

Chapter Twenty-Two:

Goals

Once you've got your Vision Board created, the next step is to turn those dreams into goals. We understand that goal setting is hard for people. It doesn't come naturally to most of us, but everything we've accomplished started out as a goal; even Chris's getting clean and sober and Debbie's quitting nursing were goals. What astonishes us is that people come up to us all the time and say that they don't set goals because they are totally fearful of not being able to achieve them. And when they don't achieve their goals, they think of themselves as failures. What really stings is when people tell us that they have never set a goal in their lives because they never wanted to disappoint themselves. Ouch! For people to be so weak-minded that they aren't willing to push themselves even a little is just astonishing to us.

Going for a Base Hit

Even if you don't achieve your goal, you aren't a failure. Think of a professional baseball player. Every time a pro goes up to bat, his goal is to get at least a base hit. But just realize that even the pros fail at least 75 percent of the time, because some of them finish the season with a .250 average. Just because a player strikes out one time doesn't mean he quits the game or goes up to bat the next time with a goal of striking out again. His goal is to get a base hit, even if it doesn't happen every time. That's the attitude we have about our business and our lives. We can take anything and transform it into a goal, and so can you!

S.M.A.R.T. Goals

We know that goal setting can be challenging. But that doesn't mean it's impossible to do. One of our mentors explained to us that goals need to be S.M.A.R.T. That is, they need to be Specific, Measurable, Achievable, Realistic, and Time-Stamped. We personally feel that the last one is the most important, because a goal that isn't time-stamped is a dream that will never become a reality—and more often than not, that dream becomes a nightmare. But that doesn't mean the first four aren't important as well.

Specific

You can't be vague about a goal. You must be concrete and specific about whatever it is in life that you want to achieve. You can't just say that you want a new car. What does that mean? What kind of car do you want? What make? What model? What color? What kind of interior? What kind of wheels? Is it going to have a

150

navigation system? Is it going to have a sunroof? What kind of engine is going to be under the hood? Is it going to have remote start? You must be specific.

Which leads us back to the Vision Board. If you have a new car on your board, take a look at that picture. Is it the precise car you want? If it isn't, then find a picture of the exact car you want and put that on your board instead. It would be even better for you to go to a dealership and take a picture of yourself sitting in the car you want to buy, then put that picture on your Vision Board.

The same is true for any of the items on your board. Make sure they are specific to what you want—the exact tennis bracelet or the exact cruise line you want to take to Alaska. The more specific, the better.

That's why we say don't try to make your Vision Board perfect. Especially with your first one, it may have to evolve a bit before it truly reflects your exact dreams.

Measurable

Being measurable relates back to being specific. You can't just say you want more money. If you find a penny on the ground, you now have more money; but that's probably not what you meant. You need to be able to measure your progress, so instead of "more money," you need to set a goal of "$1,000 more per week." That way, you know exactly where you are in relation to achieving your goal.

Achievable

While we do believe that you can dream of doing anything, a goal has to be something that can actually be accomplished, even if the odds seem against it. For instance, Spencer West of Canada lost his legs when he was five years old, but he always dreamed of climbing Mt. Kilimanjaro. After exhaustive training, he managed to reach the 19,341-foot-high summit using only his arms and hands! His dream, while difficult, was achievable. If he had a dream of growing new legs and then hiking to the summit on them, well, that's just not achievable at this point in time.

Realistic

The next part of a S.M.A.R.T. goal is that it must be realistic. Now here is where people get bogged down. They assume something isn't realistic, so they give up without even trying. A lot of times this happens when a goal is set too high at the onset. For example, if you are earning $500 a week, to set a goal of earning $500,000 by next Tuesday isn't realistic. Now it may be realistic to set a goal of $500,000, but it's not realistic to achieve that overnight.

Setting a goal of doubling your income to $1,000 a week—that's realistic.

Let's take another example. If you are in your fifties and you want to become a ballet dancer, you might be able to take lessons and learn how to dance and perhaps even be able to perform; but it's not realistic to dream about becoming the lead ballerina in the Bolshoi Ballet if you are fifty-five and have never danced a day in your life. Realistic to learn to dance? Absolutely! Realistic to become the lead in the Russian ballet? Not so much.

Time-Stamped

We believe this is absolutely the most essential part of setting goals. If you just want something someday, someday may never get here. And even more than that, if you don't time-stamp your goal, you are likely to give up. So if you want that black convertible Corvette with the leather interior and a manual transmission, you have to set a (realistic) date when you will purchase it. The date gives you focus and creates a target for you aim at.

So what happens if you don't reach the goal on time?

Goal Adjustment

You adjust. Every goal is adjustable. When this was first explained to us, our mentor had four goals that he had put on a business card and laminated. He went through those goals with us one at a time: "You see this one? I hit it right on target. You see this one? It took me an extra nine months, but I still made it."

We have date-stamped goals that didn't quite hit the mark. A prime one was Debbie's goal to achieve a level of promotion in her business by January 31 of one year. She didn't hit it by the target, but she did hit it two weeks later. Together, we had a goal to become the number four income earners in our company. It was on our Vision Board for at least three years before we accomplished it. We never gave up, and each year that we didn't make it, we would set it as a new goal. Because it was on our Vision Board, it was something we saw multiple times each day.

As long as you are striving for something, you have the ability to achieve it. But if it is just up in the air, a one day someday, then one day someday may never come.

Revising Your Strategy

That doesn't mean you just shrug and go on if you don't make a goal. When that happens, review your actions. Most of all, make sure that you have been taking action to make the goal a reality! Then see how your actions stack up. If you had a goal to make $10,000 this week but you only made $6,000, at least you know you are on the right track. Maybe the goal was a bit too ambitious for this point in time, or maybe there is something you could do better. But at least you know whether you are on track or not. Give yourself credit for what you have accomplished, and don't beat yourself up for what you haven't done. Remember, *It's Never Too Late!*

Then, once you've seen where you are, readjust your goal. For our new consultants, we always give them a first goal of a monthly paycheck of $1,000. If they don't hit it right away, then the next month's goal is $1,000. They just keep moving the goal to the next month until they hit it. And then they change the goal to $2,000 and so on until they reach their ultimate goal.

Set and Reset

The whole idea of achieving goals is learning to set and reset. Part of the whole growing and learning concept is to never quit. Instead of saying, "Well, this didn't work. I knew it wouldn't. There's no point in trying. I might as well give up," you say to yourself, "Let's reset and keep moving forward."

Remember, when we quit, we lose. If we give up, we've lost. Unfortunately, that's what some people have done in life. They tried to reach the stars and didn't make it, so they just quit. And they didn't just quit at shooting for the stars; they quit at life. They quit before they could have that new and different life they once dreamed about.

155

Missed Goals

We've had goals we didn't reach. And maybe we've set goals that we might never achieve, but that hasn't stopped us from continuing on to some other goals.

Sometimes we didn't reach the goal because it wasn't realistic, but more often it was because we realized it really wasn't a real goal. Here's an example: We had a 100-foot yacht on one Vision Board. When we put it there, Debbie had said she didn't really want to own such a yacht, but she wanted to be able to take her family and friends out on one. We kept it on the board for a while, but we never really took any steps toward achieving that dream, so it didn't materialize.

Time went by, and we decided to get married. Because of Hurricane Ike, all the usual places to get married had been destroyed and the place we found was a 110-foot yacht on Clear Lake. On December 31, 2008, we had more than a hundred of our friends join us on that 110-foot yacht to watch us get married.

Several months later, we looked at the Vision Board and said, "Well, lookie there. We had all of our friends and family sail with us on that yacht when we got married! Get the Sharpie and mark it off."

The reality is that about 95 percent of everything we've put on our boards has come to pass. The ones that haven't were because they were things we never really wanted badly enough. They were things we thought we wanted, but when it came right down to it, they weren't the sort of thing that kept us awake at night. They were "it would be nice" goals instead of the "I absolutely, positively am going to have that" sort of goal. We now understand that when we missed a goal, it was because we didn't bring the power of our minds to it fully and completely.

Which is the next topic we want to share with you—the Power of the Mind.

"If you have built castles in the air, your work need not be lost; that is where they should be. Now put the foundations under them."

— **Henry David Thoreau**, *Walden*

I know my goals, and I review them regularly to be sure they are helping me achieve my life purpose. My goals are specific, measurable, achievable, realistic, and time-stamped.

Chapter Twenty-Three:

Power of the Mind

Three quotes have greatly influenced us as we have made positive changes in our lives. The first is from the nineteenth-century American poet Ralph Waldo Emerson: "A man is what he thinks about all day long."

The second is from the great industrialist Henry Ford: "Whether you think you can or think you can't, you're right."

And the third is from our favorite book, *The Secret*: "Your power is in your thoughts, so stay awake. In other words, remember to remember."

The Power of the Made-up Mind

The one thing these quotes all have in common is that they remind us of the Power of the Mind. There is nothing more powerful than the made-up mind. This is so important that we want to say it again: There is nothing, absolutely nothing, more powerful than the made-up mind. When you make up your mind to do something and believe in yourself completely, nothing can stop you.

But the important thing is that, at some point, you have to believe in yourself. If you can't believe in yourself, no one else will either. We don't watch TV because there is too much negativity on it, and we don't want to have negative thoughts invading our minds all the time. But we do watch the show *Shark Tank*. On that show, hopeful entrepreneurs present their new ideas to a panel of five investors, the "sharks," to try to convince them to invest in their new idea.

We watch this show not to see the ideas that the contestants are pitching, but to see how they react to the five billionaires to whom they are presenting their ideas. You don't have to watch very long to realize that if the contestants don't believe in themselves, they aren't going to get the money. If they come in all cocky and sure of themselves but quickly get defeated when they get confronted or shot down, they won't get the money. It's those people who are confident, who believe in themselves and their ideas even if they are challenged and confronted by the panel, that get funding. *Shark Tank* is a great example of how what we think influences how we act and react.

Believe in Yourself

We have both learned through life's hard knocks that you have to believe in yourself for others to believe in you. It's the same principle that you have to love yourself first before others will love you. After all, the commandment says, "Love your neighbor as you love yourself." It doesn't say, "Love your neighbor, but don't love yourself."

If you want to make real changes, at some point you have to stop and take a good, hard look at yourself in the mirror. You have to see yourself for who you are and recognize that each one of us has both good and bad qualities. If you focus your mind on the good, that's what you will get. If you focus on the bad, that's what you will get.

The Story of the Two Wolves

There's a great Cherokee legend that really exemplifies this principle for us:

> A young boy came to his grandfather filled with anger at another boy who had done him an injustice. The old grandfather said to his grandson, "Let me tell you a story. I too, at times, have felt a great hate for those that have taken so much with no sorrow for what they do. But hate wears you down, and hate does not hurt your enemy. Hate is like taking poison and wishing your enemy would die as a result. I have struggled with these feelings many times.
>
> "It is as if there are two wolves inside me. One wolf is good and does no harm. He lives in harmony with all around him and does not take

offense when no offense was intended. He will only fight when it is right to do so, and in the right way.

"But the other wolf is full of anger. The littlest thing will send him into a fit of temper. He fights everyone, all the time, for no reason. He cannot think because his anger and hate are so great. It is helpless anger, because his anger will change nothing. Sometimes it is hard to live with these two wolves inside me, because both of the wolves try to dominate my spirit."

The boy looked intently into his grandfather's eyes and asked, "Which wolf will win, Grandfather?"

The grandfather smiled and replied, "The one I feed the most."

Our Lives Reflect Our Thoughts

No matter who we are talking about, this is true for all of us. One thing that Chris tells the consultants who come into our business is that when he was in jail the last time, he took a long, hard look at his life. He literally couldn't look in a mirror because he didn't have one, so he just looked inside himself. When he did that, he realized he wasn't in jail because of the system or the police. He was in jail because of his thoughts, actions, and reactions.

162

It was the same for Debbie. She wasn't working sixty hours a week because someone was forcing her to be a workaholic. She was doing it because that was the way she thought she had to live to get ahead.

For both of us, our lives were a direct reflection of the way we were thinking. We are millionaires now because we changed our thoughts, which changed our actions, which changed the way we react. We've both learned that it is okay to take a deep breath and think before you speak or react.

Sometimes people ask us if everyone has the ability to control their minds and change their lives.

The answer is simple: Absolutely!

We don't think God made us different. We don't think God gave birth to us and said, "Yeah, I like you guys, but I really don't like those other people over there." We don't believe God prejudges people and says, "Okay, I'll believe in you and give you the ability to improve your lives, but you over there—you're stuck and can never change."

It's just our own thinking, our own minds, that create the differences.

The Keys to the Power of the Mind

There are two keys to tapping into the Power of the Mind that we have found to be absolutely essential.

The first is that you must be willing to listen. If we had not been willing to listen when people brought the Ambit business to us, we wouldn't be where we are today. We had to put aside our own ideas and listen with an open mind.

The second is to surround yourself with positive people. There's an old saying, "Water seeks its own level." Well, the same is true of thoughts. If you are with people who are negative all the time, you are going to be negative. If you are around positive people, you will become more positive. This was totally true in Chris's life. He tells people it was his thoughts that did him in. He says that he was a self-abused person his entire life—a person who would rather wreak havoc on himself than enjoy his life. His negative outlook created negative circumstances, which led to a completely negative life.

We feel so incredibly blessed that we were able to come to the realization at about the same time that everything we do and everything we can become is because of our own mindset. We were able to reinforce that mindset in each other and encourage each other as we made the necessary changes in our lives. We are able to be a positive influence on each other every day, and we strive to be a positive influence on every single person we meet in our lives.

Once you realize just how powerful your mind is, then you will begin to see changes in your life. At each moment of your life, each time you make a decision or a choice, you begin to understand that what you do right then will make a difference either positively or negatively.

Leap of Faith

When we began our current business, we both had to take a leap of faith. Neither of us had done anything like this before, but we both made up our minds that it was now or never. We made our decisions, and then we committed to doing everything we could to follow through on that. We know that if we can continue to work together, we can continue to help other people. And that's what really motivates us.

We can't stress it enough: Nothing is more powerful than the made-up mind. But you get to choose what you make up your mind to do.

We'd like to close this chapter with this thought: Do you realize that God gave us humans more power than the angels? I don't believe that the angels had a choice. They were destined to be good. They could never choose between right and wrong. But God gave that choice to human beings. He gave us more power than He gave the angels. But it is up to us to determine what we do with that power.

Do we choose to be good, or do we choose to be bad? Do we choose to help, or do we choose to harm? That's our choice. God will let us live our lives the way we personally choose to live them. The choice is up to us. That's the most powerful gift anybody could ever be given—but each individual must decide what to do with it.

Current Outlook

When it comes to the Power of the Mind, it really doesn't matter what you've done or accomplished in the past. It all depends on your current outlook. You have to want to change. You must have the desire and determination to rid yourself of negative thoughts and focus on the positives of life. In other words, you must learn to be grateful for all things—which is the topic of our next chapter.

"In your hands will be placed the exact results of your thoughts; you will receive that which you earn; no more, no less. Whatever your present environment may be, you will fall, remain, or rise with your thoughts, your vision, your ideal. You will become as small as your controlling desire; as great as your dominant aspiration."

— James Allen

Today I choose to think only good, uplifting, positive thoughts. I banish all negativity from my life and surround myself with positive people who inspire me.

Chapter Twenty-Four:
The Secret Behind The Secret

We live by the book *The Secret* by Rhonda Byrne. It has changed our lives, and we believe that it can change yours as well. Just remember to be open-minded when you read it.

We discovered *The Secret* when we first began working together, long before we were even a couple. We shared the CDs, trading off each week with each other and talking about the principles we were learning. Those CDs are still in our cars today, and we still listen to them regularly.

What *The Secret* did for us was to allow us to say, "I can do that!" We took the teachings and applied them to our lives. We believe making that application was a major component in changing our lives, which is why we want to share the book's ideas with you.

The Basics

If you aren't familiar with *The Secret*, these are the basic premises:

We have the power to create the kind of life we want by harnessing the Power of the Mind through the Law of Attraction.

The Law of Attraction is a hypothesis that says "like attracts like." Wikipedia explains it this way: "By focusing on positive or negative thoughts, one can bring about positive or negative results. This belief is based upon the idea that people and their thoughts are both made from "pure energy," and the belief that like energy attracts like energy."

There are three steps to using the power of your mind that are based on the following quote from the Bible: "And all things, whatsoever ye shall ask in prayer, believing, ye shall receive" (Matthew 21:22, KJV). The steps are:

1. "Ask the Universe (God, the Source, your Higher Power) for what you want." In essence, get your desires very clear in your mind. (Do not limit yourself to any possibility.)

2. Believe. "Act, speak, and think as though you have already received what you've asked for." When you emit the frequency of having received it, the Law of Attraction moves people, events, and circumstances for you to receive.

3. Receive. "Feel the way you will feel once your desire has manifested." Feeling good now puts you on the frequency of what you want.

While there is some controversy about the science behind *The Secret*, we only know that it has worked for us. As we have changed the way we thought and felt, we have changed the circumstances of our lives. It has worked, so we have used it in our lives. We believe that if something works, you don't need to analyze it to death. You just need to apply it. That's what we've done with *The Secret*.

You Become What You Think

Because of the principles we learned in *The Secret*, we know beyond any doubt that you can become whatever you think. You get what you focus on. If you focus on wealth, you'll get wealth. If you focus on addiction, you'll get addiction. If you focus on a loving relationship, you'll get a loving relationship. Wherever you put your focus, that's where the results will begin to materialize.

The Secret taught us to dream, to visualize those dreams and then turn those dreams into goals. Chris's first dream/goal was to not still be living with his parents when he turned forty. Debbie's first dream/goal was to cut back on the hours she was working. From that, the dreams and goals evolved until we finally had the dream/goal of living in a luxury waterfront home.

But we aren't ready to sit back and pat ourselves on the back. We know that if we do that, we will begin to slip back into old patterns—which we'll discuss in another chapter that deals with flipping the switch.

Behind *The Secret*

But before we get to that, we have a secret to share with you. There is a secret behind *The Secret*.

It's so simple that you might not even think it's worth considering, but it is massively powerful. That secret is gratitude. As the book says, "One of the most powerful uses of gratitude can be incorporated in the Creative Process to turbocharge what you want."

Every day when we wake up, we take a few minutes to express our gratitude. We do it in the form of a prayer. But whether you thank God, the Universe, your Higher Power, or someone or something else, taking the time to be grateful will change your life.

Now you may be saying, "It's easy for you guys to be grateful. You've got it all—the house, the cars, the vacations." While it's true that we have many things we are grateful for, we are no more grateful for them than we were when Chris got that soccer ball or Debbie got to quit her evening job. You don't have to wait until you've achieved a certain level before being grateful. You can be grateful right now, in whatever circumstances you find yourself, because we all have things to be grateful for.

Are you breathing? Be grateful.

Do you have fresh water and indoor plumbing? Be grateful.

Can you see? Be grateful.

Do you have a roof over your head (even if it isn't your dream house)? Be grateful.

Be grateful for every success you have. Celebrate each step you take that leads you toward your ultimate goal. Be as thankful for the penny you find on the sidewalk as you are for the $10,000 check.

Why? Because according to the principles that are taught in *The Secret*, the Universe/God/Higher Power doesn't differentiate between the thankfulness you feel for the penny or the thankfulness for the $10,000. Gratitude is simply gratitude, and the more grateful you feel, the more you will have to feel grateful for.

Gratitude Affirmations

When you get in the habit of expressing gratitude, it will become second nature. But while you are learning, we suggest that you choose a few affirmations of gratitude. Write them on your Vision Board where you can see them all the time. You might even want to write them out and carry them in your wallet or purse so that you see them each time you buy something.

A few that we like include:

1. I am grateful for everything I have and everything I will receive today.

2. I am grateful for love, goodness, and prosperity in my life.

3. I am grateful for the challenges that I have experienced because they make me stronger and a better person.

4. I feel joy every day.

5. I see beauty wherever I look.

6. I am grateful for good health and for my family's good health.

Reiterating once again what the book, *The Secret*, says: "Be grateful for what you have now. As you begin to think about all the things in your life you are grateful for, you will be amazed at the never-ending thoughts that come back to you of more things to be grateful for. You have to make a start, and then the Law of Attraction will receive those grateful thoughts and give you more just like them."

No matter how long or short your prayers are, they are never wasted in God's economy.

I am grateful for every part of my life. I look for things to be grateful for and find them wherever I look.

Chapter Twenty-Five:
Flip the Switch

One of the reasons we have changed our lives is that we learned how to "flip the switch." We'll explain what that means, but first think about a light switch for a minute. You flip it up and the light comes on. You flip it down and the light goes off. The electricity behind the switch is always there, but you control whether the light is off or on.

Now consider that we all have thoughts every day. In fact, we have between 50,000 and 70,000 thoughts a day. That's more than thirty-five thoughts per waking moment!

Negative or Positive

How many of those thoughts are negative, and how many of them are positive? Before you say you don't know, take a look at your life. Your life will tell you if your thoughts are negative or positive. If your life is going the way you want it to, if you are achieving the things you want to achieve, if you have the lifestyle you want to live, then your thoughts are probably mostly positive. But if things aren't the way you would like them to be, we can almost guarantee that the majority of your thoughts are negative.

Your thoughts are like the electricity behind the light switch. The electricity is always there, but you have a choice whether to turn on the light or not. The same is true of your thoughts. You are always going to be thinking, but you have the ability to decide if the thoughts are going to be positive or negative. In other words, you must choose to flip the switch in your mind.

The way you think influences what is going to happen to you. You can start to derive a purpose from your thoughts. You always have the choice to think either positively or negatively about any situation.

Your Thoughts Are Your Choice

Here's an example. We are in the business of providing energy. Sometimes we have the best rates on the planet and sometimes we don't. It's just the way of the business. So let's say that our company raises its rates by a penny. Now we no longer have the best rate in an area. At that point we have a choice. We can freak out and worry that we are going to lose customers because of a rate increase, or we can take the longer view and realize that if we had to raise rates, all the other companies are going to eventually raise their rates as well.

If we get upset, our thoughts are going to become negative and it's guaranteed that we are going to project that to our customers. Now we might lose some customers due to the rate increase, but we will definitely lose more customers as a result of a negative attitude—not to mention that we will also find it much more difficult to attract new customers.

So what do we do when we hear about a rate increase? We flip the switch in our heads and say, "It's no big deal. We can deal with this. It will be fine."

We know that isn't always easy. For a time, we got comfortable and stopped working to help other people. We just sat back and began to enjoy all that we had accomplished. We had reached our initial goals and began to think we had arrived. Guess what? Our business began to suffer. Our income began to go down. We began to feel more dissatisfied with our lives, even though we still had met our goals.

All of this happened because we had gone from a positive, helping mindset to a self-centered, self-satisfied one. We had stopped dreaming. We had mistaken the achievement of certain goals for the ultimate dream.

So we flipped the switch and got back on track using the tools and techniques that we know work. We remembered our motto: People helping people. And we reminded ourselves that those aren't just words—they are our way of life.

We had to get back to physically building our business daily, because we were holding others back by our inaction. We needed to have our vision stretched again.

We knew that it was time to get back to it so that we were helping more people get to where we are today.

We knew we had to flip the switch.

It's Up to You

You are the one and only person who can flip that switch. No one else can do it for you. You have to do it on your own. That's why it is so important to learn to dream again and to realize that dreams have to involve other people. You can't just dream about me…me…me. If you do that, you'll fall into a negative trap, because selfishness is one of the most negative states of mind you can ever be in.

Some of the people we have helped have asked if they can talk a little bit about their journeys, so in the next section, we are going to let some of them explain how they have changed their lives. But even though all of these people are with us in our company, you don't have to be involved in network marketing to achieve the life of your dreams. It isn't the business; it's the mindset.

Adjust Your Mindset

Everything depends on your mindset.

Let's say there's a woman who has an enjoyable forty-hour-a-week job, and she has a goal to get a brand-new Ford Escape. There's no money to get the Escape, but she really wants one. So she flips a switch and asks, "What can I do to earn more money?" Maybe there's a part-time job or a skill she can use. Whatever it is, flipping that switch brings the realization that she can physically do more than she gives herself credit for. She doesn't have to settle for only the income her job provides.

So let's say this woman has a real knack for making quilts. She can sell her quilts for top dollar, but in order to do that, she needs a way to get to the quilt shows. The car she has isn't reliable, but she knows a new Ford Escape would be just what she needs.

At that point, she has a focus for her goal. She has a reason to get a part-time job somewhere so she can buy that Ford Escape. Then she can begin to take her quilts to shows. Maybe she can even enter her quilts in competitions. Eventually she may be able to quit that part-time job and earn the same money by selling quilts.

But if she didn't have the goal, she might never show the world that she knows how to make award-winning quilts. So she flipped the switch in her mind and began to focus on all the positive reasons why working a part-time job is the best thing she can do right now.

You always have the ability to flip the switch. You just have to make up your mind to do it.

"Change your thoughts, and you change your world."

—Norman Vincent Peale

I know that I have the ability to flip the switch in my mind so that I can stop thinking negative thoughts and replace them with positive ones. Today I choose to think only positive thoughts.

Chapter Twenty-Six: The Power of Persistence

Napoleon Hill was an author and an advisor to Franklin D. Roosevelt. One of his most famous sayings is, "Anything the mind of man can conceive and believe, it can achieve." He wrote a book called *Think and Grow Rich*, which is one of the best-selling self-help books of all time. We consider it one of our favorite books along with *The Secret*. In it, he tells a story called "Three Feet from Gold" about a man named R. U. Darby.

Vein of Gold

Darby was struck by gold fever in the Colorado gold rush days, and he and his uncle staked a claim on a strike they had found. They worked the mine, and when the first car of ore was smelted, they learned they had tapped into one of the richest mines in Colorado.

They immediately began digging with all the enthusiasm that comes from knowing they would soon be wealthy men. Unfortunately, the vein of gold tapped out. As Hill says, "They had come to the end of the rainbow, and the pot of gold was no longer there!" They kept

183

drilling for a while, but there was no more gold to be found, so they quit.

They sold their equipment to a junk man and took the train back East. That junk man consulted a mining engineer who showed him that the vein would pick back up just three feet from where Darby and his uncle had given up. So the junk man began drilling and, sure enough, he found the gold and became a wealthy man.

Two Lessons

This story taught us two important lessons. First, it doesn't matter what we are talking about; you can't do anything in life by yourself. You will have to have a team of people—the right people. Once the junk man got the mining engineer on his team, that's when he struck it rich. It wasn't until we discovered network marketing and surrounded ourselves with positive, enthusiastic, hopeful people that we became positive, enthusiastic, and hopeful.

The second lesson is one that we would have everyone learn: Never Give Up! Remember that Darby and his uncle failed because they gave up too soon. Three feet too soon!

Never Give Up!

Thank God Michael Jordan and Walt Disney and Thomas Edison and Lucille Ball and J. K. Rowling never gave up! Think about it.

Michael Jordan tried out for his varsity basketball team during his sophomore year of high school, but failed to make the cut.

Walt Disney lost the rights to his first cartoon character, Oswald the Lucky Rabbit, and had to start over with Mickey Mouse. When he tried to get financing for his dream of a family amusement park, he was turned down by 640 banks.

Thomas Edison failed over and over in his attempts to produce an electric light. He famously said, "I have not failed 10,000 times. I have not failed once. I have succeeded in proving that those 10,000 ways will not work. When I have eliminated the ways that will not work, I will find the way that will work."

Lucille Ball was repeatedly fired from shows and told that she wasn't funny before she became the first woman to run a major television studio.

J. K. Rowling, the author of the enormously successful Harry Potter books, was rejected by twelve publishers before she sold *Harry Potter and the Philosopher's Stone*. Her book sales now top more than $400 million.

What would have happened if any of these people had given up three feet from their vein of gold? What if they had listened to those who told them they weren't good enough or that they were too old or that they shouldn't even bother trying?

And then there is Abraham Lincoln. We recently got this email that really spoke to us about the importance of persistence.

Abraham Lincoln

Probably the greatest example of persistence is Abraham Lincoln. If you want to learn about somebody who didn't quit, look no further. Born into poverty, Lincoln was faced with defeat throughout his life. It has been said that he lost eight elections, twice failed in business, and suffered a nervous breakdown. He could have quit many times—but he didn't; and because he didn't quit, he became one of the greatest presidents in the history of our country.

Lincoln was a champion and he never gave up. Here is a sketch of Lincoln's road to the White House:

- 1816: His family was forced out of their home. He had to work to support them.

- 1818: His mother died.

- 1831: Failed in business.

- 1832: Ran for state legislature and lost.

- 1832: Also lost his job; wanted to go to law school but couldn't get in.

- 1833: Borrowed some money from a friend to begin a business, and by the end of the year he was bankrupt. He spent the next seventeen years of his life paying off this debt.

- 1834: Ran for state legislature again and won.

- 1835: Was engaged to be married, but his sweetheart died and his heart was broken.

- 1836: Had a total nervous breakdown and was in bed for six months.

- 1838: Sought to become speaker of the state legislature but was defeated.

- 1840: Sought to become elector but was again defeated.

- 1843: Ran for Congress and lost.

- 1846: Ran for Congress again; this time he won and did a good job in Washington.

- 1848: Ran for re-election to Congress but lost.

- 1849 Sought the job of land officer in his home state but was rejected.

- 1854: Ran for Senate of the United States and lost.

• 1856: Sought the vice-presidential nomination at his party's national convention but received fewer than 100 votes.

• 1858: Ran for U.S. Senate again and lost once more.

• 1860: Elected president of the United States

Saved by Your Dreams

Anyone can make a list of things they'd like to have "someday" or push play on the self-help video or even read a book like this. That doesn't require any persistence. But when you are laughed at, when you are told that you aren't going to make it, the only thing that is going to save you are your dreams and goals. If you don't have a time-stamped dream—in other words, a concrete goal—you're done for. When the first sign of difficulty comes along, you're going to quit. But if the goal is more important than anyone else's opinion, you'll show up and keep showing up.

We see it all the time in our business. When people are mocked for getting involved in direct sales or when they are turned down by the first ten or twenty people they call, they just put down the phone and go back to their old lives. They quit before they have even begun.

If you quit, you are an automatic failure; but you can never be a failure if you pick yourself up and keep on trying. The only true failure is giving up.

So we ask you, how far are you from your vein of gold? Are you going to quit before you reach it, or are you going to exercise the power of persistence?

Remember, the choice is always yours.

"It's always too early to quit."

— Norman Vincent Peale

I will not quit until I have achieved the life I know I deserve.

Chapter Twenty-Seven:
Our Purpose

Our goal in working our business and writing this book is to help as many people as possible understand that they don't have to settle. We settled for way too long. Sometimes we even settled for less than mediocrity. Just because we did it doesn't mean that you need to put yourself through the same pain and misery.

We have learned that when we live by a dream, we have a purpose in life; and as long as we have a purpose, our lives will have meaning. We have also learned that everything we have is a by-product of helping others. The more money we make personally means that we've helped more people make an income that can transform their lives.

It always comes back to helping other people. You can only have so many new cars or houses, so the ultimate goal is to help other people.

Each day, no matter what you do in life, you have two choices: you can either help people or you can hurt people. There is no in between. So every day that we wake up to do something for our business, we are helping people. But the day when we decide not to work in our business is the day we begin to hurt those who have come to trust and depend on us.

Our purpose is to help you achieve an outstanding life.

Always remember: *It's Never Too Late!*

"Live the change you want to see in the world, and you will become the change the world needs to see."

— **Chris and Debbie Atkinson**

I know I am here for a reason, and every day I strive to make a positive difference in the world.

Dreams Do Come True!

We know that if you follow the principles we've learned, your dreams will come true. We said that we have achieved at least 95 percent of what we have put on our Vision Boards, but we want to share one incredible story with you that shows just how powerful dreams, Vision Boards, and the made-up mind can be.

About three years ago, we sat down and got extremely real with each other about what we wanted. You see, we had gotten a little comfortable. We had moved into a nice house and remodeled it. We had the nice cars, and we took the nice vacations.

We had reached some goals and dreams, so we were thinking we were doing pretty well. In our heads, we were there. We had arrived. We weren't working very hard. We were taking days off, we weren't going to as many meetings, and we weren't contacting people. We weren't focused on helping others. We were focused on ourselves.

One morning we realized that we didn't have any goals. So we sat each other down and said, "We know better." We asked each other, "What is it that you want?" It took us a few days to get our dreams back in line, but at the end of that time, we made a brand-new Vision Board. We picked out the house we would like to have, the cars we would like to own, the dreams we would like to accomplish. And just like we tell others, we got out the pictures and the glue and the scissors and created a new Vision Board. We took the new board and put in on the front window where we could see it all the time.

Now fast forward a couple of years. Chris landed one day after a three-week trip, and Debbie picked him up at the airport and said there were three houses to go see. So we went and looked at these three houses. One of them we just fell in love with, and we knew that we had to buy it. We made the offer, bought the house, and moved in.

The day we moved in, Chris took his camera and walked all the way down to the end of the 200-foot-long fishing pier. He turned around and took a picture of the house, walked inside to the printer, and printed out the picture he had just taken. He handed it to Debbie, and she gasped and said, "Oh my goodness!" Chris freaked out and said, "What's wrong? What's wrong?" Debbie picked up the picture of the house and ran to our Vision Board. She held the picture right underneath the picture of our dream house that had been there for three years. The match was about 95 to 98 percent accurate. We had bought the house we had dreamed of owning!

If you believe it, you can achieve it. But we don't just want you to take our word. We have invited our sons and some of the people we work with to talk about how their lives have changed and how their dreams have come true.

We are letting them tell their stories in their own words. Our hope is that their stories will inspire you to believe that *It's Never Too Late!*

Ryan Atkinson

When I was younger, I really didn't get to see my dad (Chris) that much. I pretty much grew up with my mom. I saw my dad struggle so much from job to job, lose houses, and live in cars. He eventually got into some trouble, and I wasn't allowed to see him at all for a while. Then he cleaned himself up, and once he found Ambit, I started seeing him become more successful. As I got a little bit older, I was finally allowed to spend time with him.

Ambit actually provided the time for us to be together, and that is really why we do this business—to have time to spend with our families. We don't have to go work forty, sixty, or eighty hours a week to provide for our family, living paycheck to paycheck; instead, we get to spend the rest of our lives together.

It's a huge difference compared to what life was like before. At one time, my dad had two jobs and earned near minimum wage at both. Then he had to quit one and was let go from the other, so he was out of money and looking for work again. He actually lived with my grandparents, so when I was allowed to visit him, he'd pick me up and take me to spend time with his parents while he went to work.

After all that, what we are doing now has been a major life change. Now we have time to spend together. I can go see him whenever I want. Now that he has time to be available, we have developed a real father/son relationship.

Of course we loved each other very much before our lives changed. But because we really didn't get to see each other at all, I felt like I really didn't know my dad even though I did get to see him every now and then. Before, he was never happy; now he always has a smile on his face. We are very close. We talk all the time. It's just a huge change from what we had before.

Joseph Aymes

When we were young, my mom (Debbie) did give us the best life possible, but at times it was a struggle. When we were really young, the power was turned off because she was not able to pay the electric bill; but she told my brother Bobby and me that something happened down the street with the transformer and it would be back on shortly. She actually had to borrow the money to get the lights turned on again. It's actually rather humorous that she gets free electricity these days.

Now we take family vacations at least twice a year, when we might have taken a vacation once every five years when we were growing up. I tell Mom that she looks so much older in her pictures from fifteen years ago than she does now. Though she loved her nursing job, I feel that she's changed because of the stress relief from no longer having to work two jobs from 7:30 a.m. to 1:30 the next morning day after day. Now she is able to just enjoy life. I believe her current lifestyle has added years to her life.

Mom has always been a person to go out of her way to help anybody, and I've always known there was something better for her. Since Ambit came along, she has helped so many other people financially with this opportunity. It has been amazing to see her up on the stage with 10,000 people in the crowd cheering for her because of everybody she has helped along the way.

The same is true of my stepdad, Chris. I have only known him for the past few years, but to see him come from where he was to where he is now has just been a life-changing event. He has a great deal of determination.

My mom—she can do anything. That is one thing I think has attracted a lot of people in Ambit. She had never done this type of business before—network marketing— but she has been so successful at it because of her work ethic and her ability to do anything.

My wife, Crystal, is a cancer survivor. When she was going through the doctors' visits, consultations, and chemotherapy and radiation treatments, I was able to be by her side during every one of them. At twenty-eight years old, I was retired from working a regular job and financially free. I had the time freedom to be with my wife during those crucial days because I didn't have a boss telling me I had to be at work instead. That's priceless!

Bobby Aymes

The biggest changes I see in my mom (Debbie) would be physical changes. She looks twenty years younger. If you look at pictures of her ten years ago, she looks older in those pictures than she looks now. She always looked tired before. Now she is able to get a good night's sleep.

Living the life she was living before, that would have been impossible. First, she wouldn't have had the money. She couldn't have afforded to miss work. The lifestyle that she and Chris live is a big change—not having to get up and clock in and out anymore, being able to take vacations when they want, enjoying a beautiful house and nice cars. It is just a pretty obvious change from the outside looking in.

I would also say Mom is happier. She has always wanted to just be able to live life, and that is what she is able to do now. Before she was working sixty to eighty hours a week; now she doesn't have to do that.

My mom is one of those people who does whatever she sets her mind to do, and nothing will get in her way. She is always willing to help someone. It doesn't matter if she has just met you or if she has known you forever.

She didn't have any prior experience in network marketing, but she just followed the system. She basically did what she was told to do—plain and simple. Most people overcomplicate the business, and that is why they aren't successful with it. Mom was just a regular, ordinary person who got hold of this and did exactly what she was told to do, and the results are exactly what they should be.

I worked twelve years as an air conditioning technician. I was used to buying off the dollar menu at the drive-thru and eating lunch every day in my work van on the job. Now, because of the success in my Ambit Energy business, I'm able to cook lunch in my own kitchen every day with my fiancée, Maria, and eat on the back deck of our home that sits on a private lake. To say that my life has changed would be an understatement.

Kevin and Rose Duncan

We learned quickly after meeting Chris and Debbie that you're in business *for* yourself, but not *by* yourself. The two of them were role models for us from the day we started working with them. They really showed us the beauty of this business, which is teamwork. In addition, their culture of people helping people has guided us in the way that we grow and build our team. We are just so blessed to have them in our lives, guiding us in our business.

199

The biggest lesson Chris and Debbie taught us is that anything is possible regardless of your background or anything else. If you take a look at the type of people they are, the kind of people they attract, and what they have accomplished from the day they started until today, they are constantly demonstrating that anything is possible. They have the ability to show people "you can do this and more." Debbie Atkinson has such a nurturing, mentoring spirit. As a former nurse, she tells people all the time, "I used to help people with their health; now I help them with their wealth." She taught us that if you can teach people this business and help them grow in it, so many other parts of their lives will improve. Chris and Debbie teach that professional courtesy is core: respecting each other, teamwork, making sure that you do for other people what is done for you, and never forgetting where you started. Through their leadership and personal growth, they have taught us that the business is the means to earn income and gain wealth, but more importantly that helping people is a way of life.

(Rose) One facet of our story makes me want to cry because now I have a little boy I wouldn't have had otherwise. When I received my first big check from Ambit, I told Kevin I wanted to have another baby. While I was in corporate America, there was always the fear that if I got pregnant, I would lose my promotions or not be considered for the next slot for manager or executive. When I realized we were making a great income in Ambit, options started to open up, including completing our family.

(Kevin) We call him our Ambit baby because he really is. If we had never had the extra income, we never would have had the guts to have him. Chris and Debbie were a big part of Rose's decision to walk away from her corporate job when we saw that there was another way to make more money that didn't include sacrificing more time with our family.

(Rose) I was really scared. You're always really scared to make a decision that is going to affect your family and your finances. To walk away from something (secure) like that, just hoping that everything is going to be okay, is big. But I took a leap of faith because of a conversation I had with Debbie at her home. She said to me, "I'll know when you're no longer at Verizon Wireless, because your Ambit Energy business is going to go up." I was scared and still a little skeptical, but I trusted and believed her because she had shared with me all the stories about when she went through this same thing. It was great of her to take the time to comfort me. She let me know she was going to support me either way. She said if I made the decision to leave Verizon, I wouldn't have to worry because she had already decided from looking at my records with Ambit that I would be fine. It was Debbie's encouragement and my trusting that she believed in me that gave me the courage. I've never regretted it since. I haven't had to look back.

Ambit gave me the chance to focus on my business, but I never would have taken that leap of faith without someone like Debbie telling me it was going to be okay.

Another important thing they taught us was to use a Vision Board. At first we thought the board was cheesy, but Chris and Debbie let us know how important it was. They talked to us about some of the littlest things they had on their Vision Board and how dreams become reality because you're constantly achieving these things. They taught us that if you don't ever put it on the board, if you don't ever dream about it, then you don't even know what you're working for. As a result, we have already accomplished so much in our lives that we are now on our fourth Vision Board. One of the first things on our Vision Board was a new Cadillac SRX, and we are driving that car now. So that was a big accomplishment we got to check off, but there were small achievements too—like having matching Tupperware! While trying to raise five kids, matching Tupperware is not a priority. But, having the extra money, knowing all our kids are healthy, and with all our bills paid, it was one of those things we wanted. Though it wasn't a necessity, it was there on the Vision Board. We also included items like braces for the kids. We used to live a "not now" life. Today we are able to say yes to the things our kids want. It's an incredible feeling for parents to be able to give your children something, then have the time to watch them enjoy it. It's just huge.

By the way, all of our kids have a Vision Board too. My little nine-year-old is putting all kinds of toys on it, but that's because she knows it's possible. My kids are reaching for the stars, and they believe more is possible because we're not telling them it's not. We're not telling them that they're probably not going to college because we can't afford it. We are not living the NO life anymore. My children know it's all possible for them, and they are just waiting for it. They have started to decide what they want for their future. I think that's awesome.

Another thing on our first Vision Board was dinner with the family. We were going days, sometimes weeks, without ever getting to sit down and have a meal together. We used to think our kids would be raised in daycare because that was normal. We thought you had to work for it if you wanted to get ahead. It was not uncommon for my parents not to be there when I was growing up. Before, we had to choose between providing a better lifestyle for our kids or being a part of their lives. It was never an option to do both. Now we have both, and it has been incredible!

We also have family vacations on our Vision Board. I don't know if you have ever traveled with kids, but it's horribly expensive. From one of our first Vision Boards, we were able to take a trip up to South Dakota to see Mt. Rushmore. Now we have replaced that trip with a bigger one to Scotland because I'm Scottish by heritage. Because of the expense, it's not a vacation you can just save up for while working a regular job. This big goal is really going to be meaningful to the whole family to try to achieve it.

Chris and Debbie teach us to dream bigger. With Ambit Energy, anything is possible. Kevin and I have coined this saying: "Ambit Energy allows ordinary people to make extraordinary wealth." As we see how far Chris and Debbie have come, we see our future in them. Early in our training, Chris asked, "Who wants what I have?" Of course, every hand went up. Then he continued, "Who's willing to do what I did to get there?" A lot of hands went down because it takes work, dedication, and commitment to accomplish the things he and Debbie have done. But once you meet Chris and hear his story, you look at your own life and think perhaps it isn't so hard. Chris's story has served as such an inspiration to so many of us—it's the fuel for our fire. Knowing that Chris was able to go from flat broke at the bottom of the barrel to the top of the industry gives us hope.

Another lesson we learned is that you have to believe in yourself and the people around you, and that's huge. Chris and Debbie teach us that people helping people is really what it's all about. It does become a way of life for a lot of people, and I think that's why it attracts such good people. We meet the kind of friends we want to be around and want to be associated with. Believing in yourself and those around you is powerful. When we first got married, in everything we did—every car we bought, every house we bought—we chose what we could afford, not what we wanted. The fact that we now own the Cadillac we only talked about four or five years ago is a testament to how Chris and Debbie have helped us really broaden our vision as far as what is possible.

Another positive trait that attracted us to Chris and Debbie is their priorities. In normal life, in the corporate world, it's your job, your family, and your faith—most often in that order. With Ambit, the people we meet and the people we are around show that it is your faith, your family, and then your job—and in that order. Chris and Debbie have been powerful mentors on life. Our family is better. Our relationship is better. Our future is going to be fantastic because of the things we have learned from them. That's what we try to do on a regular basis, not only with the people we meet and our team, but even with our kids— we try to teach them to believe that anything is possible, and now one of our kids wants to be a game designer.

When we are kids, grade school teachers make us write autobiographies about what we want to be when we grow up. But gradually, as we move through life, things happen with our parents or our finances so that our childhood aspirations eventually disappear. Most of the time we end up doing what we're doing because of what happens in life. It's great to be able to show people that they still have the ability to do what they want, to do it when they want, and to become what they've always dreamed of being.

Dundy Aipoalani

I am an international airline pilot, and I started my Ambit business in the state of Pennsylvania. I will tell you that my sole reason for success is Chris and Debbie Atkinson. I live in Warren, Pennsylvania, about ten miles south of the New York border. Due to my schedule, I had maybe one day a week to work on the business. We were doing business presentations in a town called Jamestown, New York, about forty-five minutes north of my house, and every single Tuesday for a year, Chris and/or Debbie Atkinson would fly to Jamestown, New York. I think the year after that, they were there every other Tuesday.

I did not have any previous networking experience when I started with Ambit Energy, so I had a lot of what I guess you'd call challenges. My wife thought I was in a pyramid scheme. She wouldn't let me talk to any of her friends for a year. But let me tell you what happened. In less than a year and a half, the passive residual income was enough that my wife was able to quit her job. About two and half months later, we were invited to become executive consultants.

I just shadowed Chris and Debbie Atkinson. Whenever they were in town, Chris would do a presentation. He would stand in the front and answer questions. I always tried to sit in the front at the meetings to take notes. Afterward, as Chris stood there answering questions for a long line of people, shaking hands, and taking pictures, I would stand behind him and just listen to everything he said. In other words, I shadowed that man.

When I first met Chris four years ago when I started, he was making $55,000 a month. Not long after that, he was making $100,000 a month. We were in Chicago doing a presentation when I sat him down and said, "Listen, I have to know how you make this kind of money. It doesn't make sense to me. We airline pilots make good pay and benefits, but we don't make that kind of money a month." I also asked him what it felt like to make $100,000 a month because I didn't know anyone who made that kind of money. He said, "Let me tell you what it feels like." He took out his phone and showed me text messages. He said, "Do you have any idea how many text messages I get, how many emails, how many cards, how many letters, how many hugs, how many times a day people tell me thank you? Do you have any idea how many lives are going to change when you get started?"

That conversation changed my perspective on what it felt like to make that kind of money in terms of what our team motto is: people helping people. I also recognized that we really have to focus on the success of others and, as a by-product of that, of course, we become successful. I obviously attribute the success I have had so far to the Ambit Energy system, but without going into specifics, Chris and Debbie Atkinson taught me how to overcome the challenges I had in order to use the system properly.

When Chris and Debbie talk in terms of changing people's lives, they say it's a must that you take the time necessary to get to know the people on your team personally. You need to spend time with them—ask their kids' names and ages, find out their favorite color and favorite food, ask what kind of activities they like to do on a personal level and on a business level. Chris and Debbie also encourage us to track where a person is in the business. If he's a marketing consultant, find out how far he has to go to become a regional consultant. If he is a regional consultant, find out how far away he is from being a senior consultant. In other words, find out how many more consultants he needs to get to the next level. Whether you have to print it out, write it out, memorize it, or whatever, take the time to learn about the people in your business. Create a list of where they stand, then call them, encourage them, ask them to go to the meetings or training—whatever they need to be doing to get to their next promotion. You must help people focus on very specific activities that will help them be successful. More than just wanting their success, it's more about helping them because they don't know how to use the system as well as you do.

Chris and Debbie say the single most important aspect of building this business is desire. When we sit down with a consultant, the very first thing we ask is, "Why are you doing this business?" It's like going to the gym. You can join the gym that has the best equipment and the best trainers, but that doesn't matter if you don't have any desire to go there and work out to change your life physically. So, the first thing Chris and Debbie talk about is connecting yourself with what the other person wants. If you make what a consultant wants important to you, then you are tapping into the source or the reason for his willingness to change his life. If a person wants to change his life, you have to find out why. In other words, you need to know what's on his Vision Board.

When we were first getting started in New York, Chris and Debbie showed up for training. They went out and bought poster boards from Walmart and gave us those little four-inch scissors you get in elementary school and some glue. They said, "Okay, you're going to have to humble yourself. We're going back to kindergarten." So we sat there with our poster boards and cut out pictures that represented the things that motivated us in life. They didn't just talk about making a Vision Board; they actually provided the materials and sat there while we made our Vision Boards.

The number one personal development book of all time that I'm aware of is *Think and Grow Rich* by Napoleon

Hill. It was written around the time of the Great Depression. If Hill wrote the number one personal development book of all time, then we should pay attention to what it says. Hill said the key is to write out what you want in life. Do you want a certain amount of money each month? Do you want to put your kids through college? Do you want to be a senator? Whatever you want, you have to write it down.

Then you say that statement out loud to yourself when you wake up in the morning and again when you go to bed. In Hill's day, they didn't have graphic designers or the ability to create visuals of their goals. It is actually more effective to do a Vision Board because those visuals speak to the subconscious quicker than a written statement. Since the Vision Board is actually more effective than the plan in the number one personal development book of all time, we of course made our Vision Board and talked about it.

I'm an airline pilot, so I fly around the world. I fly to the best vacation spots in the world. So to me, going on a five-star trip is not a big motivation because it's like work to me. But my wife sat me down one day and said, "I don't know how you're going to do this, but you're going to get me to Puerto Rico." We put it on our Vision Board; it was a stated goal. Chris and Debbie talk about the millionaire mindset, and they stress setting goals. Once we set that Vision Board goal, we actually went on that five-star trip!

So, setting a goal, putting it on your Vision Board, reminding yourself, and making sure your eyes see it every day is essential. Maybe your board will be on your refrigerator. Debbie had hers initially on her bathroom mirror where she saw it when she brushed her teeth. It doesn't matter where it is or how beautiful it is. The important point is that your eyes have to see it every day. It speaks to your subconscious, which gets things growing in a way you can't understand, and that leads a person to change his life.

In closing, if there's one thing I would encourage you to do, it's making your focus or goal not necessarily changing your own personal life but helping other people change theirs. It's been proven that if your desire to change your life is selfishly motivated, that desire can only take you so far. There are only so many obstacles you are willing to overcome. But if you're willing to change your life because you want your kids' lives to change, or because you are motivated to help other people—if your focus becomes other people—that is a deeper and stronger reason to overcome obstacles.

If someone asked me to describe the most important lesson I've learned from working with Chris and Debbie with regard to changing your life, I would say it's taking the focus off of your life and placing it on the lives of others. As a by-product, you are going to help yourself as well as others.

211

Julie and Jim Brosious

One of the most important, life-changing lessons we learned from Chris is to have the ability to dream past our current income level. Most people will only dream of a bigger and better life that is within their comfort zone or within their current income level. We don't normally dream outside of that box. Chris has taught us that, in order to grow in life or have more things, you have to dream bigger. You basically have to think about your life as if you were already where you want to be. You need to think with the end in mind regarding your goals and what you want to achieve, then work toward that goal.

One of the ways Chris taught us to dream was with a Vision Board. Initially, we thought it was kind of silly, but we are actually on our third one now. A Vision Board, a dream board, consists of putting goals on paper. For us, it started with that as we basically set goals in the business that would help us get to what was on that Vision Board. So having those goals helped us to work backward. We asked ourselves what we needed to do on a yearly, monthly, weekly, and daily basis to achieve each goal. It made our daily activity pretty regimented when we made sure we were doing something every single day to build our Ambit business. That is how we reached our goals.

It was amazing to us that we were checking things off that Vision Board, from cars, to snowmobiles, to a mountain vacation, a beach vacation, and certain financial

212

goals. All of these things were on our Vision Board, and then Chris asked us, "Now what?"

So the next Vision Board and the most recent one included a cabin in the mountains as a second home. We struggled with that at first because we didn't have a picture on our Vision Board. We voiced it, but Chris said, "Well, you have to put it on there." I said, "Well, I don't know what I want it to look like yet. I don't know what I want my kitchen to be." He said, "You can't know that until you start putting it down." He challenged us and asked, "Do you believe that you can achieve that?"

And that's all it took. It went right on that Vision Board, and less than a year later, it's done. We are living there a lot of the time. So, I really believe in the Vision Board. It makes you dream bigger when you have to sit down and put something on it that you haven't achieved or that you don't have. That's the purpose of it.

But our board doesn't include just houses or material possessions. We have words like "believe," "dream," and "helping others" on that board. We have goals on there that pertain to the business as well, so it is full circle, a balance. We list specific goals in the business, such as X-number of people in a certain part of our business to promote to the next level. We really believe in balance in life, so there are goals like helping our children to be able to purchase their first home by helping them in their businesses. Our kids are both senior consultants, so now our board contains family goals as well as team goals.

One thing that we would tell people is to believe in yourself and believe that all things are possible. To do that, you have to have a belief in yourself and the dream. And you have to learn to dream.

Chris and Debbie are really big on that. It's amazing what you can achieve and what you can help others achieve. One way is by teaching duplication. In business, Chris and Debbie taught us to duplicate leadership—to learn what they did, to do it ourselves, and then to teach others. We have done that not only in business but also with our children. It has made a big difference in our family because we have taught our kids, who are in their twenties, to think differently.

(Jim) The greatest lesson I have learned from Chris and Debbie is to put yourself out there to help people be more. I was used to the old way of having my own businesses and doing what I needed to do to make my businesses successful. I used to own a small liquor store here in New York. We live in a village of about three thousand people, and I also had a chimney sweep business, kind of like Bert in Mary Poppins, so I went from roof to roof sweeping chimneys. In addition, I also had a water distribution business. I sold five-gallon jugs and water coolers and all the equipment that went along with them.

But Chris and Debbie made us realize that this business is just about helping everybody else. So, basically I think what they do is teach you to build relationships. You have a lot better relationships with people by doing that because you get to know people better than you do in the traditional business sense.

Using the Vision Board, Chris and Debbie really open your mind and help you look back to those days when you dreamed of what you wanted and what you wanted to work for. I feel like I did when I was a kid with dreams and goals and aspirations of what I wanted to do. With traditional businesses, those kinds of dreams fade away as you get older. This business revitalizes that part of your life. The Vision Board helps you to visualize what you want from your life. Chris and Debbie always say to include even things you just want, like a new car. But on the Vision Board, you have to actually see the car. You have to know what color it is and what the interior looks like. You can't just want "a new car." Opening your mind to the possibilities kind of brings back your youth. You're doing things that you thought you should be doing all along as you are becoming successful in the business.

Steve Sunday

The biggest lesson I have learned from Chris and Debbie is to stay focused on your dreams and on the reason you started in the business.

That's what I tell people when they join our business: to always keep their original goal in mind. All of us at one point hit the submit button to start our Ambit business. At that point, there is a reason we did it. Chris and Debbie have always said to us, "Just stay focused on the reason you started. Obviously as you go along in Ambit, your business is going to grow, and your dreams are going to grow right along with it." In the beginning, Chris told us that we weren't dreaming big enough. We were just thinking mortgage payment, car payment with the cars we had, etc. He even saw our Vision Board early on and said, "You're not dreaming big enough there either!" So we revamped our Vision Board and started thinking about the big picture. Now my wife, Connie, instead of driving the Honda CRV she was driving when we started the business, is driving the Mercedes she always wanted. That happened because of our Vision Board and because we stayed focused and kept our eye on the prize.

That was the biggest lesson we learned from Chris and Debbie—just keep reaching for the stars and pretty soon you'll be surrounded by stars.

We started our business three years ago. I was a self-employed electrician. When we looked at Ambit, I had no retirement plan in place; so I saw this as a way out for myself. Now, three years later, I have walked away from that electrical business. My wife works for the post office, and my next goal is to get her retired.

For us, our reason for joining Ambit has always been goal oriented. In the beginning, it was our goal just to make the car payment; then we added the mortgage payment, and then it became both. Now Ambit is paying every bill we have, and it's all because we stayed focused on those goals. We just kept setting our goals a lot higher. Every time we reached a goal, we set a new goal. Now life is much easier all the way around for us because we don't have to think about money. I was told early on that it's like breathing. When you get the wind knocked out of you, all you're thinking about is that next breath. When everything is normal, you're breathing without thinking about it. It's the same with money. When you have enough, you don't think about it. When you don't have enough, it's all you think about.

One other thing is that I now think about how I can help everyone with whom I come in contact. Before, with my electrical business, I would just do what I was there to do. I would get paid for it, and by the end of the day, I was absolutely tired of talking to people. Now I can't wait to talk to people. I go out of my way to talk to people. It's just a different mindset. You're helping so many people change their lives that it becomes almost like an addiction. You want to go out and help more, and in turn that makes you want to help more. My outlook on life is totally different. Before, I felt people were just there because I needed them to make a living; now I want to help them change their lives. It's not about the money. It's about helping people change their lives like ours have changed.

I truly did believe I was going to work until I died, but now I have found a better way. It's all about leveraging your time. Early on, Chris told us there are two ways to create wealth: either leverage your money or leverage your time. The time aspect is what caught my attention because, again, I could only work so many hours a day, so many days a week, and so many weeks in the year—but now we have been able to leverage that time.

If I were to leave you with one thought, it would be this: there is a better way, an easier way.

Sara Markos

The biggest thing that Chris and Debbie taught me, the huge shift for me, was when they taught me about goals. I grew up working in corporate America where nothing was done on a really emotional, passionate level. You did your work just to get the job done. You had goals for deadlines and reports to get in, but Chris and Debbie just completely opened up another whole world when they started teaching me about goals with an emotional connection attached to them.

The process of working on my Vision Board and sharing it with them and putting deadlines on things and making my board so that it gave me goose bumps when I looked at it put me into action. Passion was there naturally versus "that would be nice to have."

I always compare it to when I placed on my Vision Board the first ultrasound picture of my first little girl who is now one. I would look at that, and it would motivate me into action. So looking at your Vision Board versus looking at something materialistic that would "maybe be nice to have but..." was one of the most important lessons I learned from Chris and Debbie.

Let me tell you a story. I have always wanted a BMW, as some of the people in my family that I really respected have had them. For whatever reason, I just loved the car. So, I had the logo of the BMW on my Vision Board in the beginning. I didn't really know what kind. I didn't know what color. I didn't know what model I wanted. Chris helped me really dig into that until I had a 528i on my board. It had a Venetian beige interior and Alpine white exterior. When I looked at that picture, I reached the point that I could smell the leather. Looking at the Vision Board and really believing in a moment when it was already mine or being so certain it was going to be mine right around the corner was something Chris taught me. Before, when I put goals on the board, it seemed so long-term. Chris really helped me understand that those things CAN be mine.

He would say, "Tell me about your house. Walk through your house and tell me about it. What kind of floors does it have? What kind of aroma is going to be in the house? What are you going to have in the kitchen? What's in the fridge?" He helped me dream a lot more to get clarity for myself about what I really wanted. The more I did that, the more excited I got. The more excited I got, the more I was moved to action. And the more I acted, the more my board started becoming reality and the momentum just kept building.

My Vision Board now is so clear. I could stand at that board for three hours and tell you about what's on my Vision Board. In contrast, my first one was something that would end up at the bottom of the paper stack on my desk. When people came over and I was cleaning up, it ended up in my shoe closet. Today, my Vision Board is in a room that I am in every single day. It is framed and nailed on the wall. It's something that I modify and edit. I know that if it doesn't make me pick up the phone to get to work every time I look at it, then there is something wrong with my Vision Board.

Passion is so huge. When you put your mind to something you can emotionally connect to, that's when the magic happens.

I would tell people to dream like they're in preschool again. Give yourself a quiet time to really take away the negativity, take away the stress, take away the day-to-day that's like Groundhog Day every day. Take all that away. Ask yourself what you would be doing with your time.

It's finding that dreaming time again. Find a time to dream. That is so hard to find these days because we are so fast-paced. You have to create an environment that allows you to be able to dream again. As crazy and sad as that sounds, people don't dream. You look at preschoolers and kindergartners and ask them what they want to be, and they say an astronaut or the president. You ask a high-schooler, and those goals are lower. You ask a college student, and they are lower yet. You ask people who have put in two years in corporate America, and their dreams have dramatically changed. The next thing you know, you are just giving up. That was my case.

Dreaming is so important. It's so easy to get caught up worrying about the next deadline, worrying about traveling, worrying about taking care of your family, and life goes on that way. Remember that life will always go on anyway, so you always need to take the time to dream. Every single day you have to look at that Vision Board. You have to live in your dreaming time, live out your Vision Board. Live it in your mind as if it is reality.

Honestly, at first I didn't take it seriously. It was more like an art and craft time. I had to humble myself enough

221

after plugging in with Chris and Debbie and thinking, "Okay, this is what they have done. This is where they are. Since that is where I would love to be, I had better humble myself enough to do this activity." My first three Vision Boards have come a long way over time, but it's a journey. That's the beautiful part about it. It comes to life over time. It's not like I sat down and made a perfect Vision Board the first time around. It was a process of bringing it to life over time and putting it together and creating it out of what my dreams really were.

My board changes because life and priorities change. My Vision Board now is so much more centered on family and helping others. In the beginning it was all about me, me, me—the beautiful mansion, the desired vacation. Now, those things are good, but my priorities are family, savings, college funds. It is just something that evolves with you and keeps you doing the activity that is going to get you where you want to be.

Dreaming is something I so overlooked because it is a process of humbling yourself, but it is so powerful and rare these days. That's what Chris and Debbie taught me.

Tim and Missy Ulinger

We've always been entrepreneurs who looked at the big picture, so we always knew we wanted something better—we just weren't sure how to get here. Now, with the help of Debbie and Chris, we are much more goal-oriented. They taught us to find goals that will help us reach our bigger goals by using our Vision Board to be very specific instead of aiming for "eventually." We set and focus on goals that push us, but at the same time we set small goals that can help lead us to the bigger goal. The bigger goal might be at the end of the year, but the smaller goal is for the next three weeks. Those short-term goals are what keep us plugging along.

One key is to truly envision a picture of where you want to be. That's where the Vision Board comes in. We started with small things like a cleaning lady and then added the bigger things. But all your goals have to be something you can visualize, and something you really want.

(Tim) I have pictures of my five kids in my car. Before (Ambit), I had three businesses as well as worked at the police department. I was working seventy-two hours a week. I just had to work more and more hours. My five kids remind me of why I am doing this. As I keep helping more people achieve their goals, I get closer to my goal of retiring from the police force.

It's so important to help others. You have to encourage others and help them set goals. Once they have goals set, then I can help them realize and achieve their goals. The more we work together, the more we accomplish.

223

(Missy) If I had to give just one piece of advice, it would be to set your goals and know specifically what you want. When you take the focus off yourself and help others put their visions in place by focusing on other people, you are inevitably going to be successful yourself.

Our motto is, "People helping other people." We really do believe in changing people's lives on a daily basis.

Epilogue

The principles we live by are not new. We discovered them through *The Secret*, but they have been known by successful entrepreneurs for many years. One of the first was Napoleon Hill, who learned the principles from Andrew Carnegie. He expressed these lessons in his classic, *Think and Grow Rich*. Rhonda Byrne, author of *The Secret*, credits him as one of her teachers.

We'd like to leave you with a selection from that book. The ideas presented here have inspired and continue to inspire us every day. (If you want to read the whole book, it is available free on the Internet.) As you read, remember that these words were written in 1937, in the throes of the Great Depression. Much of what they prophesied has already come true, and they remain as true, as important, and as valid today as they were more than three quarters of a century ago.

So *Think and Grow Rich*!
(public domain)

The imagination is literally the workshop wherein are fashioned all plans created by man. The impulse, the DESIRE, is given shape, form, and ACTION through the aid of the imaginative faculty of the mind. It has been said that man can create anything which he can imagine. Of all the ages of civilization, this is the most favorable for the development of the imagination, because it is an age of rapid change. On every hand one may contact stimuli which develop the imagination.

Through the aid of his imaginative faculty, man has discovered, and harnessed, more of Nature's forces during the past fifty years than during the entire history of the human race, previous to that time. He has conquered the air so completely that the birds are a poor match for him in flying. He has harnessed the ether, and made it serve as a means of instantaneous communication with any part of the world. He has analyzed, and weighed the sun at a distance of millions of miles, and has determined, through the aid of IMAGINATION, the elements of which it consists. He has discovered that his own brain is both a broadcasting and a receiving station for the vibration of thought, and he is beginning now to learn how to make practical use of this discovery. He has increased the speed of locomotion, until he may now travel at a speed of more than three hundred miles an hour.

The time will soon come when a man may breakfast in New York, and lunch in San Francisco. MAN'S ONLY LIMITATION, within reason, LIES IN HIS DEVELOPMENT AND USE OF HIS IMAGINATION. He has not yet reached the apex of development in the use of his imaginative faculty. He has merely discovered that he has an imagination, and has commenced to use it in a very elementary way.

The imaginative faculty functions in two forms. One is known as "synthetic imagination," and the other as "creative

226

imagination." SYNTHETIC IMAGINATION: Through this faculty, one may arrange old concepts, ideas, or plans into new combinations. This faculty creates nothing. It merely works with the material of experience, education, and observation with which it is fed. It is the faculty used most by the inventor, with the exception of the one who draws upon the creative imagination, when he cannot solve his problem through synthetic imagination.

CREATIVE IMAGINATION: Through the faculty of creative imagination, the finite mind of man has direct communication with Infinite Intelligence. It is the faculty through which "hunches" and "inspirations" are received. It is by this faculty that all basic or new ideas are handed over to man. It is through this faculty that thought vibrations from the minds of others are received. It is through this faculty that one individual may "tune in," or communicate with the subconscious minds of other men.

The creative imagination works automatically, in the manner described in subsequent pages. This faculty functions ONLY when the conscious mind is vibrating at an exceedingly rapid rate, as for example, when the conscious mind is stimulated through the emotion of a strong desire. The creative faculty becomes more alert, more receptive to vibrations from the sources mentioned, in proportion to its development through USE ...

Both the synthetic and creative faculties of imagination become more alert with use, just as any muscle or organ of the body develops through use. Desire is only a thought, an impulse. It is nebulous and ephemeral. It is abstract, and of no value, until it has been transformed into its physical counterpart.

Epilogue

While the synthetic imagination is the one which will be used most frequently, in the process of transforming the impulse of DESIRE into money, you must keep in mind the fact that you may face circumstances and situations which demand use of the creative imagination as well.

Your imaginative faculty may have become weak through inaction. It can be revived and made alert through USE. This faculty does not die, though it may become quiescent through lack of use. Center your attention, for the time being, on the development of the synthetic imagination, because this is the faculty which you will use more often in the process of converting desire into money.

Transformation of the intangible impulse, of DESIRE, into the tangible reality of MONEY calls for the use of a plan, or plans. These plans must be formed with the aid of the imagination, and mainly with the synthetic faculty … Begin at once to put your imagination to work on the building of a plan, or plans, for the transformation of your DESIRE into money.

Detailed instructions for the building of plans have been given in almost every chapter. Carry out the instructions best suited to your needs, reduce your plan to writing, if you have not already done so. The moment you complete this, you will have DEFINITELY given concrete form to the intangible DESIRE. Read the preceding sentence once more. Read it aloud, very slowly, and as you do so, remember that the moment you reduce the statement of your desire, and a plan for its realization, to writing, you have actually TAKEN THE FIRST of a series of steps, which will enable you to convert the thought into its physical counterpart.

The earth on which you live, you, yourself, and every other material thing are the result of evolutionary change, through which microscopic bits of matter have been organized and arranged in an orderly fashion. Moreover—and this statement is of stupendous importance—this earth, every one of the billions of individual cells of your body, and every atom of matter, began as an intangible form of energy. DESIRE is thought impulse! Thought impulses are forms of energy. When you begin with the thought impulse, DESIRE, to accumulate money, you are drafting into your service the same "stuff that Nature used in creating this earth, and every material form in the universe, including the body and brain in which the thought impulses function."

As far as science has been able to determine, the entire universe consists of but two elements—matter and energy. Through the combination of energy and matter has been created everything perceptible to man, from the largest star which floats in the heavens, down to, and including, man himself.

You are now engaged in the task of trying to profit by Nature's method. You are (sincerely and earnestly, we hope) trying to adapt yourself to Nature's laws, by endeavoring to convert DESIRE into its physical or monetary equivalent. YOU CAN DO IT! IT HAS BEEN DONE BEFORE! You can build a fortune through the aid of laws which are immutable. But, first, you must become familiar with these laws and learn to USE them.

Through repetition, and by approaching the description of these principles from every conceivable angle, the author hopes to reveal to you the secret through which every great fortune has been accumulated. Strange and paradoxical as it may seem, the "secret" is NOT A SECRET. Nature herself advertises it in the earth on which we live, the stars, the planets suspended within our view, in the elements above and around us, in every blade of grass, and every form of life within our vision. Nature advertises this "secret" in the terms of biology, in the conversion of a tiny cell, so small that it may be lost on the point of a pin, into the HUMAN BEING now reading this line.

The conversion of desire into its physical equivalent is certainly no more miraculous! Do not become discouraged if you do not fully comprehend all that has been stated. Unless you have long been a student of the mind, it is not to be expected that you will assimilate all that is in this chapter upon a first reading. But you will, in time, make good progress.

The principles which follow will open the way for understanding of imagination. Assimilate that which you understand, as you read this philosophy for the first time, then, when you reread and study it, you will discover that something has happened to clarify it and give you a broader understanding of the whole. Above all, DO NOT STOP, nor hesitate in your study of these principles until you have read the book at least THREE times, for then, you will not want to stop.

About the Authors

Debbie and I have really never quite figured out if she is the Yin and I am the Yang, or if maybe I am the Yin and she is the Yang. We have completely different backgrounds. For instance, Debbie helped to run a family business for years. She then worked her way up the corporate ladder in the banking industry and later went back to college and obtained her nursing degree in record time. I, on the other hand—well let's just say that I was in college for a total of six and a half years with no degree to show for my time. To add to the disparities, Debbie has barely received a speeding ticket, while I always had a room reserved at the county jail. We are different in so very many ways.

Debbie and I believe that it is precisely this diversity of our backgrounds that make us "fit" so well together. Debbie has taught me a tremendous amount about responsibility, honesty and more. I have brought an "it's never too late or too dark" attitude to our marriage and a "you can believe in people until they believe in themselves" mentality to our outlook on life.

However, the greatest thing our togetherness and marriage has brought about is our family. When we met, I already had a son and Debbie had two boys. You should see these three together when you begin to talk movies, cars, football, and especially business! Debbie's boys are now engaged and/or married, and their wives are something special. We cherish them all! Finally, while Debbie's beloved parents passed away years ago, our entire family is still so attracted and attached to my parents, who recently celebrated 67 years of marriage at age 87 each. We may not be the model family, but our love continues to grow!